Scenes
FOR WOMEN
by Women

Also edited by Tori Haring-Smith
Monologues for Women, by Women
More Monologues for Women, by Women

Scenes
FOR WOMEN
by Women

EDITED BY

Tori Haring-Smith

HEINEMANN
Portsmouth, NH

Heinemann
A division of Reed Elsevier Inc.
361 Hanover Street
Portsmouth, NH 03801–3912
http://www.heinemann.com

Offices and agents throughout the world

The author and publisher wish to thank those who have generously
given permission to reprint borrowed material:

"Tripping Through the Car House" by Regina Porter. Copyright ©
by Regina Porter. Reprinted by permission of William Morris Agency,
Inc. on behalf of the Author.

Library of Congress Cataloging-in-Publication Data
Scenes for women, by women / edited by Tori Haring-Smith.
     p. cm.
    Includes index.
    ISBN 0-325-00067-0
    1. Acting. 2. Dialogues. 3. Women—Drama. 4. American
drama—20th century. I. Haring-Smith, Tori.
PN2080.S255   1998
812'.50809287—dc21   98-22962
                                                        CIP

Performance rights information can be found at the end of the book.

Editor: Lisa A. Barnett
Production: Elizabeth Valway
Cover design: Tom Allen/Pear Graphic Design
Manufacturing: Louise Richardson

Printed in the United States of America on acid-free paper
02 01   DA   2 3 4 5

Contents

Subject Index

Art and Artists

Careers

Family Relationships

Female Friendship

Generation Gap and Growing Older

Heterosexual Relationships and Marriage

Historical Subjects

Illness and Death

Attias, Perfect Light
Evans, Flappers
Harrington, Mercy
Jacker, The Parting of the Ways
Kramer, Things That Break
Loomer, The Waiting Room
Svich, After the Wake
Svich, A Smoke and a Line
Traina, Winnie and G
Tuan, Organic Form
Yankowitz, A Knife in the Heart

Lesbian Love and Relationships

Bacharach, Boulder Rock
Eisenstein, Marla's Devlotion
Gabow, Time Zoned
Valentine, Southern Belle

Mother/Daughter Relationships

Caruso, Shamanism in New Jersey
Lewis, Little Rhonda
McGhee-Anderson, Mothers
Sterne, Strains of Papa's Violin
Sterrett, The Moebius Band
Traina, Winnie and G
Tuan, Organic Form
Wilson, A Tragedy: San Francisco
Yondorf, Thirteen Rites

Mysticism and Spirituality

Eisenstein, Marla's Devotion

Preface

"Women Don't Say Things Like That . . ."

There are more women than men on the face of this earth. There are more women than men in Actors' Equity, the professional actors' union. There are more women than men in most theatre audiences. ("Women buy the tickets" is a common marketing mantra among theatre managers.) There have been more women than men in every acting class I have ever taught. In fact, there are so many more women than men wanting to act that it's now common (in colleges and universities, at least) to cast women in men's roles. The American theatre is bursting with women who want to act and women who want to watch them act. Why, then, are there so few roles for women compared to the many roles available for men? Why don't we see more female characters on the stage? And why is it so rare to see scenes with only women on stage?

One obvious reason is that most of the plays produced today were written by men. This is true in community theatre, on professional stages, and in college and university productions. This is not to say that men never write good roles for women; but since playwrights tend to write about what they know best, most male playwrights write about men's worlds. Female characters appear in those worlds, of course, but usually in the company of men. Scenes between two men or between a man and a woman allow for a male point of view. Such scenes are familiar to male writers—they have literally been there. Writing scenes between two women is as foreign to their experience as writing scenes about cultures they have never experienced—even as an outsider. Writers can always use their vast imaginations to create worlds, animate characters, or express feelings they have never personally experienced, but working from personal experience gives art its living fire.

In women's plays, it is naturally more common to find two or three women alone on the stage. This is the world women know. But women's plays are not being widely produced. And why is that? There are certainly lots of women out there writing plays—good plays—that languish in literary managers' offices and in desk drawers. Why is it so rare for them to be staged? Many words have been expended trying to explain this phenomenon, and it's still an enigma. Maybe the tradition of producing men's work is just too hard to break. Maybe it's a case of the "old boys' network"—male directors and artistic directors feel more comfortable producing the work of their male colleagues. Men's stories seem inherently more true and interesting to them. Maybe it's a corresponding bias in male theatre reviewers that makes the male perspective seem more important to them and hence officially more successful. Maybe the tradition of producing male playwrights persists because artistic directors these days are reluctant to take risks on *any* new voice.

I suspect that even more important than tradition, however, is the perception that men write universally appealing plays, while women write works that appeal only to women. In my work as a literary manager, I don't know how many times I've seen a play removed from consideration because it was "a woman's play." On the other hand, I have never heard of a play rejected because it was "a man's play"—unless it had only male roles, in which case its exclusively male perspective was perceptible. The male perspective seems universal because we live in a society where our myths, our stories, our religions, our songs, our art are all dominated by the male point of view. And for this reason male perceptions of reality seem "normal." They seem to be "true" portrayals of the human experience. We've gotten used to this point of view and so it seems unmarked by gender.

For this reason, when women express their gendered perceptions of the world, they are often considered "insane." Think of Virginia Woolf, Alice James, Emily Dickinson, Sylvia Plath. In the nineteenth century, many women like these were imprisoned or voluntarily fashioned their own imprisonment because their worldviews were not acceptable to others. They literally made no sense to those around them. These days we don't imprison women for seeing the world differently than men, but we do insist that their views are not universal. And so we imprison them as artists. We do not recognize their voices publicly. In the theatre, this means that most actresses play female characters that were created by men, and most female spectators watch stories of human interaction written by men. And so, the myths are perpetuated.

Given this hostile environment for women's stories, why do women keep gravitating toward a career in the theatre, with its alternating moments of ecstasy and rejection? Paradoxically, even as it excludes women's voices, the theatre seems to offer women a place where it is publicly acceptable for them to speak. Women who have trouble making their voices heard in day-to-day interaction may welcome the chance to speak their minds through the mask of a character. And because our culture accepts a woman's public display of certain emotions (grief, maternal love) more easily than it does a man's, it may be easier for women to show their vulnerability and feelings on stage. On the other hand, we must remember that female characters, as constructed by men, often display only a limited range of emotions—those acceptable in "polite" society. I remember a particularly poignant moment in a playwriting seminar when we were discussing a woman's play about two sisters. The script was realistic but raw and at times obscene. In the midst of the feedback session, one male student in the class burst out, "But women don't say things like that. They don't!" How interesting that he felt his perception of women must be more accurate than a woman's perception of her own world.

All of this is to explain why I felt a need to put together this collection of scenes written for women by women. Women writers certainly need to have their work read, and women who want to act may prefer to perform characters created by writers who have "been there." The writers in this collection speak from inside the woman's perspective. They have not only heard women talk, but they also know what women say and do when they are alone, when they do not have to conform to society's sense of what a women should be, when there are no men present. Of course, some of their behavior seems completely "normal." Other pieces may be further from your personal experience. But all of these pieces present a vision of the female experience as seen by the female writer.

The characters you will meet here are quite varied—they differ in class, age, sexuality, race. And they talk about everything—cancer, Clint Eastwood, college, art, sex, murder, birth, jigsaw puzzles. Because acting classes and auditions usually require realistic acting, most of these selections are realistic in style. The three pieces by Sherry Kramer and Caridad Svich, however, offer women an alternative performative style.

Because you may find these scenes useful in a variety of venues—acting classes, auditions, competitions, and performances—I have ensured that the anthology includes a wide variety of scenes. For example, I have included some relatively short pieces as well as some longer ones. The shorter scenes crystallize relationships quickly, while the longer ones allow relationships to develop and change. In most of the scenes, both characters undergo a marked journey from one emotional or intellectual state to another, providing a balanced focus on the characters. Only one or two scenes are intentionally designed to feature one of the two characters. Finally, most scenes are two-handers; although five—those by Sherry Kramer, Lisa Loomer, Heather McDonald, Alice Tuan, and one by Caridad Svich—have three characters.

Although most of the writers represented here have had

their work produced in New York, in regional theatres, and internationally, these particular pieces are not readily available elsewhere. At the end of the book, there is an appendix of scenes written by women for women that appear in readily available scripts. I hope that the pieces in this book, and those listed at the end will serve as a testimony to the exciting and varied possibilities for presenting the lives of women, as seen by women, on stage. Once you have heard the voices of these strong writers, I hope that you will want to bring their work into your classes, onto your stages, and into your lives.

Introduction

Tips on Preparing a Scene

Selecting a Scene

The first thing you need to consider in choosing a scene is your purpose. Do you want to find a character that seems familiar to you so that you can be comfortable at an audition? Or are you looking for a piece for an acting class that will challenge you to explore a new kind of character, situation, or dramatic style? Does the scene need to balance other scenes and monologues you are performing as part of a showcase or audition? The answers to these questions will guide you in assessing the subject and style of the scene, whether you want it to feature one character or present a balance between the two, and how long the scene needs to be. In most audition and showcase situations, you will also want to find a scene that will be new to your audience. You don't want your audience to compare your version of Juliet to the many others they've seen. You want them to see your work on its own terms.

Any scene you choose should send your character on an emotional journey. The character should go from one emotional state to another—grief to joy, confusion to enlightenment, resignation to anger. Scenes in which characters feel only one emotion throughout the interaction can seem flat when they are taken out of the context of the play in which they were written. Look to see if the course of the character's journey makes sense to you, and if it is motivated by events that occur during the scene rather than those that precede it. Of course, lots of scenes are motivated by memories, but the scene will be more present, more alive if the character's responses to those memories are motivated by onstage events.

Remember that the scene should draw attention to you and your partner, not to itself. Therefore, try to find scenes that do not require complicated props, set pieces, or costumes. You need to concentrate on the acting—not the technical aspects—as you prepare the scene. And, in scene work, you don't want to be upstaged by a roaring fire or a fancy pair of sunglasses. Even though a scene springs from the interaction of two or more characters, it must not be too context-dependent if it is going stand on its own. That is, the scene needs to make sense and be important in its own right—not because of its function within the play as a whole. Many exciting scenes cannot stand on their own because in isolation they do not reveal the characters fully or they make too many references to offstage characters. If a scene is well chosen, it should not require any introduction beyond the title of the play.

Most important, however, you need to find a personal connection to the piece so that you can bring yourself to the character. You need to understand the character's emotions and be passionate about her concerns. After all, you are going to have to explore this character in depth and then generate enough energy to make her live for your audience. In some cases, actors are drawn to characters because they have undergone similar experiences. If the character is talking about death, and you have recently lost a loved one, you may be able to share something of yourself—your grief—through bringing the character to life. Acting is, after all, about sharing yourself. That's one reason why actors must learn to be vulnerable and to relax. When you perform, your audience wants to know who you are, as well as who you can be. Your choice of a character often reveals your self, so choose carefully.

Preparing and Rehearsing the Scene

Reading and Research
The first step in preparing a scene is understanding your char-

acter. In most cases, this means that you will need to read the play from which the scene is taken. You may even want to read other plays written by the same author to give yourself a sense of the playwright's "world," her recurrent concerns and situations. Of course, since your audience will probably not have read the entire play, you cannot rely upon it to explain your characters. You read in order to comprehend the characters fully, but in performance you must make the characters stand on their own. If you cannot obtain a copy of the play, you can still perform the scene, but try to learn all you can about the writer and the characters. In some cases, you may also need to do research on specific concerns, such as an illness or a historical period that may be relevant to your character.

Asking Questions

Preparing a scene is different from preparing a monologue. You must understand not only your own character, but also your scene partner's character and your relationship to her. Here are some questions you will want to address—both alone and with your partner—through careful reading of the text, improvisation, and conversation.

- What are the given circumstances of the scene? How long have the characters known each other? What significant events have shaped their relationship so far?
- What happened immediately before the scene? (In some cases, this may be answered by reading the play; in other cases you will need to invent the action that forced the first line of the scene to be said.) How well do these characters know each other—so well that they can communicate even without words, or do they have to work in order to understand each other?
- If the subject of the scene is an event in the past, what is the present reality of the characters?
- What is the relationship of the characters and how does it change during the scene? Trace the journey of each character and the journey of the relationship. If there is a

conflict in the scene, how is it defined? Where is the climax of the scene?

- What does your character want at the beginning of the scene? What different kinds of strategies does she use in order to try to reach her goal? How does her success or failure affect what she wants by the end of the scene?
- What does your scene partner's character want at the beginning of the scene? What different kinds of strategies does she use in order to try to reach her goal? How does her success or failure affect what she wants by the end of the scene?
- What kind of language does your character use? Why? What is the most important line in the scene?
- Who makes the action happen in the scene? Who pushes whom? Do the characters know how to push each other's buttons? How to annoy each other or give each other pleasure? How do they use this knowledge to manipulate one another? If they don't know each other well, how does their ignorance affect their attempts at communication?
- What is the vocal and physical life of your character?

In exploring answers to these kinds of questions, you will want to read and reread the scene. Most of the answers will be found in the language and action on the stage. Also, remember that you are not looking for the "right" answer. There is never one "right" answer to the nature of a character. You are looking for the answers that make emotional sense for you and your partner. If you have seen someone play this role or a similar one, do not try to reproduce their performance. Don't try to be Diane Keaton in *Crimes of the Heart* or Elizabeth Taylor in *Who's Afraid of Virginia Woolf?* Approach a role with a fresh point of view.

Establishing Beats and Scoring

One of the best ways of looking at a character in depth is to break the scene into beats, paraphrase each beat, and explore the character's evolving objective. Some people call this kind of close reading *scoring* a character. If you have taken acting classes, you have undoubtedly done this kind of work already. But always remember that you want to trace your character's objectives—her needs and desires—in terms of *active* verbs. You should think, "She wants *to escape* from her mother" or "She wants *to seduce* her neighbor" or "She wants *to put* her friend *at ease*." Try to avoid verbs of telling ("She wants *to explain* herself" or "She *questions* her friend's story") since they usually do little more than describe the dialogue of the play. Also avoid verbs that describe states of emotion or being ("She *feels* sad" or "She *is* confused") since these verbs do not inject action into a scene. Scenes in which characters merely emote are rarely interesting; they usually seem flat and/or self-indulgent. An important part of scoring is paraphrasing—especially if the language of the play is archaic, highly stylized, or highly inflected by dialect or jargon. You want to know what your character is saying.

As you look carefully at your character, don't hesitate to admit when you are unsure of what she is feeling or doing. Explore these questions with your scene partner. And don't rush to a conclusion and try to force the scene to fit that conclusion. You want to make choices—but they should be comfortable ones. If your choices are right, the scene and its language should make more and more sense as you go along. If you are feeling as if you are straining to make the language fit the objectives you've established, then try another set of objectives.

Establishing a Shared Reality
When you are alone on stage, delivering a monologue, you are in complete control. You can establish the given circumstances as well as the character you are addressing. In a multi-character scene, however, it is essential that everyone on stage agrees about the reality of the situation. This means more than agreeing upon the given circumstances for the scene. Of course, you need to agree about how and where these two

people met, how well they like each other, and so on. Together, you want to decide what actions immediately preceded the first line of your scene and what will happen after the scene concludes. But you also need to make collective decisions about style—determining whether a fourth wall is in place or whether one or both of you can acknowledge the presence of the audience.

Establishing a shared reality consists not only of shared decision making, but it also means being present for and listening to each other during each performance of the scene. You and your partner must share the living moment together. If you are both alive in the scene, it could change subtly at any point. If your partner is, say, just a little angrier than usual or if she suddenly finds something in the scene funny, you must respond to that new action. Throughout rehearsal and performance, it is essential to listen to one another carefully.

Many actors use improvisation to help establish a shared reality. You may decide to improvise a scene from the past, exploring how your characters interacted when they were much younger or at a crucial time in their lives. You may also want to improvise the scene you are acting. If you begin the improvisation with the characters as they are at the top of the scene, then paraphrase your lines and just let the characters develop, you can see how the scene goes when you are not supported by the precise words of the playwright and a predetermined sense of how the action will progress. You might find that a fight becomes a love scene or vice versa. Such discoveries can lead you to fresh interpretations of scenes or to a deeper understanding of subtext. Improvisation is helpful because it allows you to find the character in yourself and your partner, not just in the playwright's words and action. When you improvise previous action, you will also have a shared past to draw upon—you will know what your scene partner's character looked like when she was a child.

Remember the most important rule of improvisation,

however: do not tell your scene partner what to do. Let her develop her character, and you develop yours. You may discuss the scene and question each other's actions, but try not to censor each other's impulses. Only in some special situations when one actor is being featured and the other merely supporting her should one actor try to limit the other one's choices.

Keeping an Open Mind

As you rehearse, remember that rehearsals are for exploring. Take risks—that's what rehearsals are for. If you are afraid of looking foolish (being too big or too small), face your fears. Allow yourself to do the scene as you fear it might be seen at its very worst. You will find that facing your fears will help them dissolve away. If you don't face them, enact them, experience your worst nightmare in the safety of a rehearsal, your fears will limit your spontaneity and make you self-protective. People censor themselves when they fear that they could be wrong. Usually, however, when people act the scene they fear they will perform, they find that they have nothing to fear. Sometimes, you even discover that your worst nightmare may be an excellent choice for the piece—you were just afraid of executing it. Don't be afraid of being quirky or bold.

Don't settle on choices too soon—keep an open mind. Try new approaches to see if the choices that were obvious to you when you read the play change at all as you actually play through it. Try starting with different assumptions about preceding action—that is, start with different definitions of the characters' relationship. If two characters seem to be getting along, what would happen if their camaraderie simply covered an underlying resentment? You may want to perform the scene in different styles—Western, opera, and so forth—to see what you can learn about the characters through different lenses.

Blocking the Scene

Deciding where, when, and how characters should move is usually a director's responsibility. However, most scene work is done without the aid of a director. Working with your partner, you can follow the same steps that a director does. Begin by walking around the space, getting used to it, finding places to sit and stand. Then walk through the scene moving as you might in real life. Don't worry about an audience—just find the physical expression of the character's relationships. Having explored the reality of the scene, you can then begin to shape that reality so that it is communicated to your audience.

Try breaking the scene into snapshots, finding a physical expression of the series of moments that constitute the play. Remember what Brecht said: the deaf and the blind should both be able to understand any theatrical performance. If your audience were deaf, could they understand your relationships through your movements on the stage? In establishing your snapshots try to layer the text and subtext physically as well as emotionally. If your character is saying she hates someone, but in truth she loves her, is there a way to show that ambivalence in her physicality? Remember that blocking involves not only standing or sitting in a given spot, but also gestures, leaning, and the direction of the gaze. You will find that space encodes power. Height gives someone power. Being close to someone usually (but not always, of course) reduces power.

If you find that you are having trouble communicating a relationship physically, try putting an obstacle—a table, a couch, whatever—between you and your scene partner. Obstacles increase tension and provide a way for actors to communicate with one another. Also remember that the audience needs to see into your relationship. If you stand close to your scene partner, you may feel right but the audience won't be able to see the action between you. In seduction scenes or fight scenes, let the audience see into the aggression or the affection. Leave physical closeness for climactic moments of extreme hatred or love.

In blocking a scene, remember that you do not need to face your scene partner every time you speak to her. People often talk while not facing each other. And finally, as you block, remember that movement is necessary to give a scene some life, but you should not move just for the sake of moving. Know why you are crossing or kneeling or sitting; every movement should convey something conceptual or psychological.

Deciding About Costumes, Props, and Set

Sometimes it is tempting to distract yourself in rehearsal by worrying about costumes or setting or props. In most cases, however, you are preparing a scene to practice or showcase your acting, not your technical skills. Costumes may help you convey a character, but your acting is more important than what you are wearing. Don't get distracted by hunting down props or set items, either. Your relationship is more important than your surroundings.

Your costumes should be simple, especially if you are performing the scene as part of a showcase or audition. The costume should not distract from the character, but it need not realize the character completely. Similarly, you may require one or two hand props, but little else to realize the scene. If the circumstances of your production allow for richer production values, then by all means indulge yourself, but remember that the power of theatre lies in the actor's magical transformation of reality for the spectator. Nails and woods and fancy clothing are secondary.

Presenting the Scene

There are certain directorial questions that you and your partner will have to answer in order to perform the scene. How will you start? How will you know when both of you are ready to perform? If the scene is part of an audition involving other scenes or monologues, how will the scene partner enter? What will you say as an introduction to the scene and how will you say it? Rehearsing not only the scene but the transitions into and out of the scene will help you feel at ease in front of an audience, even if they are just the friendly members of your acting class. I have seen too many good scenes undercut by a sloppy exit at the end of the work.

On the day of your performance, try not to establish expectations. Although you have been rehearsing the scene for several weeks, try not to picture past rehearsals. Don't expect a certain reaction to any of your lines. Just relax your body and your mind so that you can be present for your scene partner. Remember that you want to respond to what she does in the present, not what she did in a rehearsal weeks ago.

Warm up with your partner before you perform. Establish your connection so that you are prepared to listen to one another and play together. You may want to recall some of the given circumstances of the scene in order to prepare for the first line. You need to connect with one another so that together you can relax and trust yourselves. Your hours of rehearsal prepared you to perform, but the most important feature of performance is presence. Unlike film, theatre always exists in the present. If you cannot find a private space to warm up with your partner, just close your eyes, focus, and take yourself through the piece in your head. Remember that even in a crowded dressing room or outside a classroom, you and your partner can find time to chat.

Special Considerations When Auditioning

If you are performing as part of a showcase or an acting class, you will probably know where you are performing and will be familiar with the space. If, however, you are using this scene as an audition piece, you should not make assumptions about the audition space. For example, don't picture the room, because you may then be surprised and have to deal with that surprise while you are acting. If you think, "Oh, I'll be up on a big stage in a two-thousand-seat auditorium," and you end up auditioning in a hotel conference room, you will have trouble making immediate adjustments. And doing so will distract you from your focus on the scene.

Don't even make assumptions about the behavior or the number of the people who will be watching you. Sometimes you will be performing for one person in an audition situation, sometimes fifty or sixty in combined auditions like Strawhat, or Midwest Theatre Auditions. And don't anticipate rapt attention from your auditors in an audition situation. They may look at you intently, they may eat while you perform (we often don't get lunch breaks), or they may pass papers or talk about you. Don't be surprised or thrown. Just do your work and let them do theirs. It is hard not to be offended if someone is talking while you perform, but keep your concentration on your own work. Remember that they may be saying, "She's perfect for the part, isn't she!"

When it is time for you to audition, you and your scene partner will be admitted into the audition room by a monitor or the casting director. In most cases, you or the casting director will have sent your picture and résumé to the director. If not, then hand the picture and résumé to the director as you enter and cross to the audition area. If the director initiates a conversation, respond politely and efficiently. Think of this as a cocktail conversation. Most directors will not initiate conversation, however. They're rushed, and they just want to see who you are.

As soon as you enter the room, seize the space. Walk confidently and know that for the next few minutes, you are in charge of what happens in that space. It is easy to experience auditions as a kind of meat market, in which you are just a number. In fact, this is often true, but you must never present yourself as "just one more actor." Take the stage, know you're important.

If you need to move a chair or set up the space, do so quickly. Then pause to be sure that the director is ready for you to proceed. In some cases, a monitor will indicate when you should begin. Introduce yourself and your work, making eye contact with the director or with as many of a large group of directors as possible. This is the only time during the formal part of the audition that you should make direct eye contact with the auditioners. Once your introduction is over, take a few seconds (no more) to focus completely on your work and then go.

At the end of your performance, wait a beat, break character, and then say, "Thank you." If, for some reason, the director wants to see more of you, you may be asked to do a cold reading or additional monologues or scenes. Always have some additional work in reserve. It is not uncommon, especially in graduate school auditions, for directors to request specific types of work. "Do you have something more upbeat?" "Can you show us a more vulnerable character?" "Do you have something in verse?" You can never be prepared for all requests, but do have a supply of work at your beck and call. If you are not asked to do additional work, don't be depressed. You may not have suited the role, or you may have been so perfect that the auditioners knew immediately that they wanted to see you at callbacks.

At the end of the audition, never comment on your own work—especially to apologize. The most important thing is to be confident and to look like you're having a good time throughout the ordeal. Don't even comment on your own work by scowling, frowning, or shrugging as you walk away.

Once you have left the audition, try not to second-guess the director. Especially if the director seemed to respond well to your work, don't begin to fantasize about what it will be like to work with that director or on that project. If you don't get the part, you'll just be doubly disappointed. Every actor needs a strong support system. You put yourself on the line daily—you are the product that you are selling—and although you may know that not everyone wants or needs your product, it is still difficult to take rejection. Remember that even famous actors face rejection everyday. Keeping faith in yourself and in those around you who will not desert you in times of need will see you through and keep you sane.

Auditioning can be a nightmare, but it can also be fun. You meet lots of different people, get tips on upcoming projects, and have a chance (however brief) to perform. Just keep reminding yourself that you are in control of your performance. No matter how good you are, you will only be right for some roles. Can you imagine Roseanne Barr as a sensitive figure skater? Keep true to your own sense of self, keep polishing your acting skills, and be sure that you have other ways of measuring your self-worth aside from getting cast in a given role.

Remembering Your Responsibility to Your Partner

When you work together with others in the theatre, it is always important to remember your responsibility to the collaboration that generates theatre. When you embark on a joint project like acting, talk to your partner or partners about why you are doing this work. What is your goal, both personally and professionally? What do you want to achieve in this work? You and your scene partner may have different goals, but you should share your reasons for engaging in this work. This kind of conversation is especially important when one actor is being featured in a scene and the other is clearly supporting her.

Once rehearsals begin, always come to rehearsal fully prepared. To do otherwise is a sign of disrespect to those you are working with. Being prepared means doing your homework (reading the play, asking yourself questions, memorizing your lines). Then, once in rehearsal, you need to be present mentally and emotionally as well as physically. Never skip a rehearsal—remember others are waiting for you. If you are unable to attend at the last minute, be sure that you get word to your stage manager or your scene partner so that she does not waste time waiting for you.

Some actors bring in a director or a friend to watch the

play and give feedback. This can be very helpful. But generally, you will need to provide your own feedback during rehearsals. How do you think it is going? Try to be honest about your concerns but supportive of your partner as well. Being supportive does not mean lying when things are not going well, but it means looking forward, planning strategies to fix problems, not dwelling on the problems themselves. Working without a director is difficult because you must generate your own criticism and your own praise. You need to find a way to acknowledge to one another what is going well and what needs work. And when the scene is over—whether in class or in a public performance—be sure you thank one another. It is always important to acknowledge each other's time and energy. After all, working together is what makes theatre such fun.

Perfect Light

DALE ELIZABETH ATTIAS

*Present day. Two women in JEN's studio in Northern California.
JEN is a sculptor and teacher, divorced, and in the late stages of
cervical cancer. ABBY is an actress from New York, mother of two
daughters, also divorced. JEN and ABBY have been best friends
since kindergarten. In the studio is an unfinished female nude.
JEN is on the phone as ABBY returns from the bathroom.*

JEN: Okay, sweetheart. I will. Bye now. *(JEN hangs up the phone.)*

ABBY: Who dat?

JEN: David. He told me this hysterical story. Do you remember
how the hospital here has those temporary walls between the
beds? So you sort of feel like you're in a single room, even
though you're not.

ABBY: Uh huh.

JEN: Well, you can hear everything through the temporary wall.
He said there's this woman in the bed next to him. She's been
calling her family all day. One after the other. She's been begging them to come see her because she's dying. And David
says they all seem to be telling her to fuck off.

ABBY: That's horrible. Let's go visit her.

JEN: I told David you would.

ABBY: Not a single person. What do you suppose she did to them?

JEN: Must have been pretty bad.

ABBY: God, that's got to be my biggest fear in life. Being old and
sick and laying there all alone in a hospital. . . . Were you
ever pissed off at me that I didn't come when you were in the
hospital?

JEN: I told you before. You came when everyone else forgot
about me. It wasn't any big deal. Really.

ABBY: I always figured that if you were still in the hospital, then you might die. If you were going to die, they'd never let you go home. So I waited till you got home 'cause that meant you were gonna live.

JEN: Are you nuts? They send people home to die all the time. You ever hear of hospice?

ABBY: They don't send anybody home. Isn't hospice like, you know, a special hotel where you go, to, you know?

JEN: Jesus, Abby, you're talking about hostels. They do what they can, then they send you home.

ABBY: Don't I feel stupid.

JEN: And here I just figured you hated hospitals.

ABBY: Huh uh. What I hate is my best friend dying. That's all. It worked, didn't it? You didn't die. You're sitting right here, drinking wine and looking oh so glamorous. And your cancer is all better. Right?

JEN: You want another glass?

ABBY: No. Don't change the subject. I said, your cancer is all better, right?

JEN: We need to talk about this, Abby.

ABBY: Why do we need to talk about anything? Your cancer is all better. Say it, Jen. Say, "I'm in remission. They haven't found anything new."

JEN: I can't Abby, honey, because it's not true.

ABBY: God damn it. Alright. So your fucking cancer has made a stupid comeback. No big. When is the surgery? This week? I know, you didn't tell me about it because you were afraid I wouldn't come, right? Isn't that it?

JEN: No. There's no surgery this week. I've decided. No more surgery.

ABBY: What?

JEN: I decided last time. If the cancer came back, then that was it.

ABBY: No!

JEN: Abby, you can't argue this with me.

ABBY: The hell I can't.

JEN: I have to do it this way.

ABBY: But if the cancer comes back, if it grows you'll . . .

JEN: Honey, the cancer is back. And it's growing. And I am dying.

ABBY *(Furious):* Shut up. Stop saying that.

JEN: I know. I know.

ABBY: Don't cluck at me. I forbid you to be anything resembling fucking understanding.

JEN: I . . .

ABBY: No, God damn it. This isn't happening. I won't . . .

JEN: You have to.

ABBY: Fuck that. Fuck that. I don't have to. I won't stand here and let you die.

JEN: There isn't anything you can do. There isn't anything anyone can do.

ABBY: Yes there is. There's something. Radiation. Bone marrow transplants. Apricot pits, for Christ's sake.

JEN: No. Not this time.

ABBY: You can . . . They can . . . Fuck this. This isn't right. You're working on that fat woman piece. You've got hair on your head. You're doing fine.

JEN: I haven't touched that piece in two months. I don't have the strength.

ABBY: What about the college?

JEN: Permanent disability.

ABBY: God damn it to hell. Just have them cut the cancer out again. I'll stay here. I'll fly the girls out and I'll get a motel and I'll stay with you the whole time. Start to finish.

JEN: No. Not this time. I wanted to see you before I got too sick.

ABBY: I . . . You can't . . . We . . . *(ABBY is crying. Big gulping sobs.)* You can't die. *(ABBY kneels on the floor by JEN's chair and wraps her arms around her friend's knees.)* You can't die. You can't do this to me.

> *(The telephone rings. After six rings, when it is clear that the phone won't stop, JEN extricates herself from ABBY, and answers. ABBY continues to weep, huge hiccuping sobs.)*

3

JEN: Hello . . . Is this Tessie? My little Tessie? It's Jen, honey. . . . Yes, dear, your mommy's here. *(ABBY shakes her head violently no.)* Guess what? Your mommy is in the potty. She had a number two. . . . Yes, she did take a book with her. *(JEN giggles.)* Well if it's going to take that long, I don't think you want to wait for her to get finished. . . . Sure, I'll give her a hug for you. Are you all ready for bed? . . . Uh huh . . . I know that . . . Okay, sweet dreams sugar plum. Good night. *(JEN hangs up the phone. She fills ABBY's wine glass and sits beside her on the floor.)* Hey, I'm really sorry.

ABBY: Sorry? How do you figure that?

JEN: Well, first there's the contraction "I'm," combining "I" and "am"—the verb "to be."

ABBY *(Gentle):* Shut up.

JEN *(Also gentle):* Make me. *(Beat)* You remember Coad Miller?

ABBY: Sure. His parents had that huge house by the Yacht Harbor.

JEN: There was some kind of party there . . . in June. It was Bastille Day.

ABBY: How can you remember that?

JEN: Because Coad and a bunch of his friends kept screaming, "Liberty, Fraternity, Equality" in really bad French accents. Don't you remember that?

ABBY: Was I loaded?

JEN: What do you think? Anyway, I ended up way out in the back of their yard with Danny Salazar.

ABBY: That Puerto Rican guy? How the hell did a PR guy like Danny end up in Westchester County?

JEN: His parents were rich, like everybody else in Westchester.

ABBY: My parents weren't rich.

JEN: Yeah, but they had been. And your grandparents were very rich.

ABBY: Don't get off the track. What happened with you and Danny?

JEN: We did it in the grass, in the moonlight, behind Coad Miller's boathouse. And he sang to me.

ABBY *(Smirks):* Sang?

JEN: Yeah. "Wooden Ships."

ABBY: Crosby, Stills, and Nash?

JEN: Yeah. *(She sings a bit of the song very softly.)*

ABBY: While he did it?

    (JEN nods.)

JEN: The whole time. It was wonderful.

ABBY: Wow.

JEN: Yeah. He knew all the words too.

ABBY: Wow.

JEN: It was really great.

ABBY: Did you, you know, come?

JEN: No. It didn't matter. The night, the grass, the song. You know.

ABBY: Yeah. What happened to him?

JEN: He came.

ABBY: You know what I mean.

JEN: I think I heard he moved to California. Something about him being a lawyer for migrant farm workers.

ABBY: Natasha asked me what the sexual revolution was the other day.

JEN: What did you tell her?

ABBY: What was I supposed to say? It's when your mommy smoked way too much dope and fucked around like crazy?

JEN: Did you tell her that?

ABBY: Of course not. I told her it was a big party but now the party was over because of AIDS.

JEN: Is the revolution over or are we just too old to get laid? Or in my case, too scarred up?

ABBY: I don't know. I've been with Charlie for thirteen long, monogamous years—alright I know—almost monogamous years. I don't know what the hell it's like out there. All I'm sure of is that it scares the living shit out of me.

JEN: I like that expression. "Living shit." Brings to mind lots of bizarre pictures.

ABBY: Which I do not want to hear about.

JEN: I don't know anybody who talks like you. All of the faculty at the college are so PC in the way they talk. Every word chosen so as not to offend.

ABBY: "Living shit" offends people?

JEN: Sure. Not me, but when you're around students every waking hour, it's easy to say the wrong thing. The little bastards get offended by the damnedest stuff. And they complain. They write letters and they go to the chairman of the department.

ABBY: Did they do that to you?

JEN: No. Somebody else at work. A guy. Really put his ass in the wringer.

ABBY: Did he get fired?

JEN: No. But the poor guy had to go to a zillion meetings, write all kinds of explanations, even an apology to the student who complained.

ABBY: That's fucked.

JEN: So everyone is overly careful. Can't offend anybody's race. Height. Weight. Baldness. Particularly can't make comments about disabilities.

ABBY: No mentioning the fact that they're stupid, talentless zeros.

JEN: Maybe it's just a way to end racism.

ABBY: Horse shit. It's a way to drive me nuts. He's short and bald and has a little dick—what's that? Vertically, folically, and penally challenged? Please!

JEN: You'll always call him a short bald guy with a little dick. Maybe you shouldn't move out here after all.

ABBY: I'll move any fucking place I like. Now, what was all that bullshit about you not having another surgery. You were kidding, right?

JEN: No.

ABBY: Dammit, Jen. Fun's fun. But you gotta be straight with me now. Is the cancer really back, or what?

JEN: Yes, the cancer is really back. There's tumors all over.

ABBY: Then when is the surgery?

JEN: No. No more surgery.

ABBY: This isn't funny. I don't get the game you're playing.

JEN: I'm not playing a game. This is it.

ABBY *(Sharp):* God damn it, Jen. Don't kid about this.

JEN: I know it's hard for you.

ABBY: Fuck. "I know it's hard for you." What the hell are you talking about? What kind of mumbo jumbo is this?

JEN: It's not mumbo jumbo. It's just the way it will happen.

ABBY: No. Absolutely not.

JEN: Yes. This is it.

ABBY: I refuse.

JEN: This is denial. I expected it.

ABBY: Screw you. Don't give me that sanctimonious "I took Psych 101 and I know all about what you're feeling."

JEN: Death is the biggest stress there is. Believe me, I know.

ABBY: How the fuck can you just sit there drinking wine telling me about some kid you fucked twenty years ago?

JEN: You asked me. And I finished my wine off a while ago.

(ABBY can't sit still. Starts pacing in the studio.)

ABBY: Oh, God. What the hell am I doing here?

JEN: Do you want to go back to the house?

ABBY: No. Yes. No. Dammit I don't know what I want.

(There is a thump, then a rumble. Then a tinkle, and the overhead light begins to sway back and forth.)

What the . . . ?

JEN: Earthquake. Doorway.

(JEN is on her feet and grabs ABBY pulling her to the doorjamb. The earthquake is over. A few items have been knocked off shelves—no serious damage. The rumbling sounds end, then the lamp slows its sway.)

ABBY *(Terrorized):* Is it over?

JEN *(Nonchalant):* Yeah. It wasn't a big one.

ABBY: : It wasn't big? You call that not big?

JEN: A four maybe. Nothing bigger than that.

ABBY: How can you be so calm? My heart is pounding.

JEN: Come on, back to the couch. It's OK to sit down now.

ABBY: No. Fuck. What if there's another one?

JEN: There will be another one. There's always another one. But probably not right away.

ABBY: Jesus. You look like nothing happened.

JEN: Nothing did happen. A couple of books fell over. No big.

ABBY: God. It was like slow motion. I was sure the whole building would collapse around us.

JEN: You can tell when they're not very big like that.

ABBY: How?

JEN: It wasn't loud. The big ones are really loud.

ABBY: How many you been in?

JEN: Tons of little ones like that. Two big ones.

ABBY: Oh man. How can you stand it?

JEN: You get kinda used to them.

ABBY: Why does anyone want to live in a place where it does that?

JEN: Hey, you've got your share of problems in New York.

ABBY: Yeah?

JEN: What about ice storms?

ABBY: Yeah, but we've got some stiff on the weather channel telling us just when the big storm will start.

JEN: Yeah, but . . .

ABBY: Don't "yeah but" me. This earthquake stuff is shit. It's a bolt from out of the blue.

JEN: No, but it . . .

ABBY: And people actually live here? The very earth under their feet goes all wobbly, and they just go stand in a doorway. That's crazy!

JEN: Next winter, when you're out there scraping the ice off your windshield, you think of me, sunning out on my deck . . .

ABBY: I'd rather scrape. You get up in the morning, and if it's winter, you're gonna scrape. Here, you don't know if you're gonna live or die from day to day.

JEN: I do.

ABBY: Hey! Cancer doesn't count. You could have tumors all over the fucking place, and still die when the roof caved in.

JEN: But it won't cave in. The house is up to code.

ABBY: I don't know that. God, the way they build stuff in New York. Just think what would happen if they ever had an earthquake there!

JEN: They're on a fault there too.

ABBY: Whose fault?

JEN: Your fault.

(A familiar routine with these two.)

ABBY: No way. Not my fault. I had nothing to do with it.

JEN: You always have something to do with it.

ABBY *(Bronx accent):* Yeah? Who says? Your mother?

JEN *(Same Bronx accent):* You making fun of my mudder?

ABBY: You making fun of my accent?

JEN: Yeah, so what?

ABBY: I'll tell you what. I'll tell you what all over da place.

JEN *(Normal voice):* God, you sound like you just got off the IRT.

ABBY: Don't you miss it? Won't you come back east once before . . .

JEN: I doubt it.

ABBY: You aren't . . .

(Beat)

JEN: Don't mush out again. This is all about closure. For everything there is a season.

ABBY: Oh Christ, she's quoting The Doors.

JEN: Not The Doors. It was The Byrds.

ABBY: No. Jim Morrison.

JEN: Huh uh. The guy with the glasses in The Byrds. What's his name. "To everything turn, turn, turn."

ABBY: Maybe you're right.

JEN: I'm always right.

ABBY: Ecclesiastes. You ever read that?

JEN: Yeah. I've read it.

ABBY: You ever get, you know. Into that?

JEN: Not born again. Is that what you mean?

ABBY: No. Not that. I was wondering if you ever, you know, prayed.

JEN: Yeah. I pray.

ABBY: You think He listens to you?

JEN: Sure. She listens.

ABBY: Why doesn't She do something then? Why?? Is She sitting around with Her head up Her whatsit?

JEN: For everything there is a season.

ABBY: And you're an autumn so we should dress you in fucking earth tones when we take you to the morgue.

JEN: A time to live and a time to die.

ABBY: A time to jerk off and a time to kiss up.

JEN: Play nice.

ABBY: Can't. I'm mad at Him. Her. Whatever.

JEN: This is the life I had. It wasn't bad.

ABBY: It isn't long enough. IT WASN'T LONG ENOUGH!
    (Pause)

JEN: So whose life is long enough?

ABBY: What about George Burns? He was older than dirt when he died.

JEN: What about Gracie Allen?

ABBY: What about her?

JEN: Don't you think we loved George Burns so much because he was always true to Gracie?

ABBY: He wasn't. He cheated on her. She was going to leave him. But she settled on a new silver centerpiece.

JEN: You're making that up.

ABBY: Nope. She said in later years she wanted him to cheat again because she needed a new silver centerpiece.

JEN: It must be true. You'd never be able to make up that part about the centerpiece.

ABBY: I don't even know what a silver centerpiece is.

JEN: Some fifties thing.

ABBY: Right.

JEN: Well?

ABBY: What?

JEN: What is it you want to ask?

ABBY: Why do you think I want to ask something?

JEN: Whenever you start showing off your astounding knowledge of Hollywood trivia, you are about to ask a big question.

ABBY: I do that?

JEN: You've done that for years. When we were in high school you'd say things like, "John, Paul, and George are all five feet eleven inches. Ringo is five feet seven."

ABBY: Doesn't everybody know that?

JEN: Then you'd ask me to let you copy my math homework.

ABBY: Really?

JEN: So what do you want?

ABBY: I want . . . I want you to tell me what to do. What do you want me to do now?

JEN: I want you to have another glass of wine. I want to slam Charlie some more. I want to listen to your strange view on the world. I want to stroll down memory lane with you a while. And then, I want you to bring the girls out to California and live out here until I'm dead.

ABBY: Jesus.

JEN: I never asked you for anything before.

ABBY: Yes you did.

JEN: But never this big. See, I'm not afraid to die. I'm afraid to die alone.

ABBY: God.

JEN: She's listening. She didn't like that line about Her head being up Her you-know.

ABBY: I'm having some trouble taking this idea in.

JEN: There won't be an earthquake while you're here.

ABBY: Are you nuts? There just was an earthquake two minutes ago.

JEN: There won't be a big one. I promise.

ABBY: How can you be sure?

JEN: I can be sure.

ABBY: Terminal cancer gives you second sight or something?

JEN: It's desperation. I will command the earth to remain still while you live in California.

ABBY: And I'm supposed to come out here to watch you die?

JEN: You won't just watch. I intend for you to be an absolute participant.

ABBY: How?

JEN: When it gets too weird, I've got this nice big stash of prescription drugs.

ABBY: I . . .

JEN: Your answer is not required right this second.

ABBY: What's . . . How . . .

JEN: Shhhhh. Hey, it'll be good for you to get away from Charlie for a while.

ABBY: Charlie who? Oh God.

(ABBY stands, and moves downstage of JEN's chair toward the female nude. ABBY hangs onto the sculpture for support. Tears stream down her face.)

Boulder Rock

JILL IRIS BACHARACH

Two women at home. SAM, *37, a divorced pastry chef, and*
ANNA, *29, a naïve businesswoman, have been lovers for seven
years.* ANNA *has recently fallen in love with another woman and*
SAM *is having an affair in retaliation.*

SAM *and* ANNA's *living room. Sofa is center stage. Kitchenette
upstage left. Reading chair and end table downstage left with a
television further stage left.* SAM *is seated in the reading chair in
a baseball cap and sunglasses—reading the newspaper.* ANNA's
hair is wet. ANNA *is kneeling on the stage right end of the sofa
drinking a liter of bottled water. It is early evening, still light
outside, sometime after dinner. The television is on a movie station and is playing the film version of* The Odd Couple.

ANNA *(To herself, but aloud):* Criminal. Seven letters. . . . *(To
SAM)* Did it thrill you to read the letters from Sachi while I
was away?
  *(SAM pulls down her sunglasses, squints, and then covers her
  eyes again.)*
ANNA: Well?
SAM: Your nose is twitching.
ANNA *(Exasperated but controlled):* Are you going to answer me?
  (SAM pulls down sunglasses. Stares. Puts glasses back on.)
  WHAT?
  (SAM says nothing.)
  Sam, I'm talking to you!
SAM *(Flatly):* Uh huh.
ANNA: Oh! That goddamn smirk! All you ever do— *(She stops in
frustration.)*

SAM: What's wrong?

ANNA: EVERYTHING!

SAM: What the hell are you getting so upset about?

ANNA: BECAUSE! *(About to "lose it")* Something's—

SAM *(Interrupts. Flat. Distracted. Toward the television):* Did you change the channel?

ANNA: Christ! Do you even hear me?

SAM: Try "voyeur." *(Suddenly)* Seven letters?

ANNA: JESUS—

> *(The phone rings. ANNA stops and looks offstage to the right. She doesn't move.)*

SAM: Why don't you get it? You know it's *her!* Seven letters. *(SAM counts out a word to herself gesturing with her fingers.)*

ANNA *(Drifting. Conflicted. Begins scratching something out of the couch pillow. Frustrated):* The machine's . . .

> *(There is a pause and then a voice is heard.)*

SACHI'S VOICE: Hello? Hellllll... ooooooo ooooohhhh? Anyone there? Are you there? Well, I'm back, sweetie. I'll be up for another hour. Call. *(There is a click and then a long beep tone.)*

SAM: Why didn't you get that?

ANNA: BECAUSE! I'm trying to talk to you.

SAM: But she's hundreds of miles away.

ANNA: So are you.

SAM *(Snaps):* What!

ANNA: You lay in bed next to me and your knees feel like knives.

SAM: Sachi's teaching you poetry now?

ANNA: SAM! For god's sake! I'm trying— I need to know where you are.

SAM: I haven't had a day off in four weeks. I just want to sit in my chair, read the paper, and go to bed.

ANNA: You changed the subject.

SAM: It's a shitty subject.

ANNA: But it's there, Sam.

SAM: Then make it go away.

ANNA *(Focusing on the pillow):* Another knife.

SAM: What?

ANNA: Do you even listen to yourself?

SAM: What did I do now?

ANNA: It takes work, Sam.

SAM: I'm tired.

ANNA *(Escalating):* And you've had a stressful day. You didn't have a chance to eat, and you—*(Controlled)* haven't had a day off. . . .

SAM: Right.

ANNA *(Angry):* And the bottom line is, you don't want to do the work!

SAM: I'm tired.

ANNA: It's boring, Sam.

SAM: Why? Because I'm not always up for a visit into the emotional psyche of Anna "Freud"? Because I'm not your little *Sachito?*

ANNA: That's not fair.

SAM: Why? Because you don't have a clever response?

ANNA: No. Because you make a statement like that and then you give me the silent treatment.

SAM: You wanna break up, don't you?

ANNA: What?

SAM: You feel stuck with me and you want to break up.

(The phone rings. They both look stage right. A beep. And then a voice.)

SACHI'S VOICE: Hi there. It's me again. Just want you to know I love you. I love you too, Sam.

SAM *(To machine):* Bitch. You'd rather be with her.

(ANNA gestures the ritualistic plunge into stomach. SAM turns a page in the paper. Silence.)

ANNA: Do you have any idea how you're torturing me? *(Beat)* It's not the affair as much as the fact that you make it so illicit—like everything—it has to be so goddamn secretive.

SAM: Contrary to popular opinion, I *know* what it means.

ANNA: I didn't mean—

SAM: You didn't mean— Fuck you. I know you're in love with her.

ANNA: I never denied that. But all I get is your sarcasm. And your silence. I need more, Sam.

SAM: Fuck you! What you mean is— you need Sachi.

ANNA *(Louder): I mean,* I need to know how you feel when you wear your sunglasses during dinner. When you turn away from me at night. I need to know who is living in our bed. Who is shutting your eyes. Who's whispering goodnight. Who's there? Who, Sam, who? . . . Because I know it isn't me. I know you don't see me. There are so many ghosts here, Sam. There's no room for me anymore.

SAM *(Interrupts):* You want to break up, don't you?

ANNA: Is that what you heard? *(SAM is silent.)* Is that what you heard?

SAM: Seven letters . . . Try "illicit."

ANNA: I'm not the criminal, Sam. Why don't you tell me what you heard?

(Phone rings. They stare at each other.)

In the Presence

SALLIE BINGHAM

The living-dining room of LOU ALDEN's house. A large, old television is strategically placed in front of a worn, comfortable armchair. On shelves, a collection of "Negro" knickknacks and a sizable library of well-worn books. A picture window, curtains drawn; on the sill, a tray of dirt. A typewriter, covered, sits on the downstage right table beside a large pile of unopened mail. Stage left, door to the front hall, with coatrack. Stage right, door to the kitchen. The telephone is off the hook and the TV is on. LOU ALDEN, an elderly, retired activist, is standing at the window, looking at the tray of dirt. In her hand is a packet of seeds. With one finger, she begins to trace lines in the dirt, then hesitates, shakes her head. She puts on her glasses and reads from the seed packet.

LOU: "Plant indoors in early spring . . ." Call this early spring? *(She peers out the window.)* Sleet, hail—and fire— *(She drops the seed packet.)* Damn seeds too small to see. Ken's job, anyway. I never did claim a green thumb. *(She begins, slowly, to put on a heavy coat.)* Newspaperperson won't throw the rag up on my porch—heaves it in the bushes. *(She is fastening her coat and at the same time she is drawn to the television; she stands looking at it as she puts on gloves. The doorbell rings.)* Good Lord! This early— *(She goes to the mantel, checks the clock, which is not running, shakes it. Doorbell rings again.)* Coming—hold your horses! *(She exits. Voices, off. LOU backs onto the stage, followed by ELLIE, a young, pregnant reporter.)* You have some nerve—!

ELLIE: This new incident—

LOU: New to you! *(ELLIE comes farther into the room, begins to take off her coat.)* Make yourself at home!

ELLIE: I won't stay long. *(She takes a tape recorder out of her brief-case.)*

LOU: Good. *(She watches with interest as ELLIE readies the tape.)* You rely on that—?

ELLIE: I take notes, too. . . . *(Handing her a newspaper.)* Brought you your paper. It was in the shrubbery.

LOU: Shrubbery! *(She glances at the headlines.)* So they did it again.

ELLIE: Same story. Mind if I sit down?

LOU: Looks like you need to.

ELLIE *(Sitting):* I'm writing about that business in '54, compar-ing it to this new trouble. Can I ask you a few questions?

LOU: I always talk to the press. It's my only defense.

ELLIE: You heard what happened last night.

LOU: I tried not to.

ELLIE: Your TV's on. *(LOU grimaces, turns it off.)* Black couple bought a little house in Shiveley. Fire-bombed around mid-night. We ran a six-inch item—

LOU: Where?

ELLIE *(Showing her):* Right here—second page.

LOU: Second page!

ELLIE: They're not too keen on blowing it up—

LOU: I thought you were in the business of blowing things up.

ELLIE: They've promised me a background piece tomorrow.

LOU: First time this happened, you weren't even hatched.

ELLIE *(Checking notes):* They never did catch the people that did it, back in '54. Instead they sent you and Ken to the pen. Nobody would buy a house, deed it over, then blow the darned thing up.

LOU: How do you know?

ELLIE: It doesn't make sense. Just a few questions. *(She turns on her tape recorder.)*

LOU *(Unbuttoning her coat):* Ask away. You won't like the answers.

ELLIE: You were crucial, in '54—

LOU: I had no choice.

ELLIE: Does that mean you regret—?

LOU: Nothing as simple as that.

ELLIE *(Consulting clippings):* You went all over the state, lecturing about the miscarriage of justice—soon as you were out of jail. Raised money by the handful! But now you wouldn't consider—

LOU: That depends.

ELLIE: On what?

LOU: The way I feel, young lady. I've got arthritis, some days I don't get out of bed.

ELLIE *(Writing):* I'll say you have health problems.

LOU: The way I feel depends on more than arthritis. . . . That thing working?

ELLIE *(Checking tape):* Yes. I tried to call you—

LOU *(Taking off coat):* I keep the phone off the hook. *(She pushes a large pile of unanswered mail away in order to move closer to the tape recorder. ELLIE notices the mail.)* I need some peace and quiet!

ELLIE: The activist in retirement.

LOU: I did my bit.

ELLIE: But Lou—there's nobody to put this new incident in perspective— *(LOU is staring at her.)* I'm sorry.

LOU: Everybody calls me by my first name—like a discount store—or a church. How long till that baby's due?

ELLIE *(Reluctantly turns off recorder):* Five and a half weeks.

LOU: First babies are always late.

ELLIE: My doctor says—

LOU: Did he figure it out on his pocket calculator? Nobody knows why they come when they do, or why they go. If you knew that, you could found a whole new religion.

ELLIE *(Switching tape recorder back on):* Are you a feminist?

LOU: Are you planning on natural childbirth?

ELLIE: My husband says—

LOU: He won't be there. It'll just be you, alone on a bed in a very small room.

ELLIE *(Consulting her notes):* Can you tell me how raising a family affected your activities in the civil rights movement?

LOU: It wasn't a family. It was a daughter. One.

ELLIE: I know.

(*Pause*)

LOU: Are you going to put that precious baby in day care?

ELLIE: We can't afford a nurse.

LOU: Can you tell me how raising a family will affect your career in journalism?

ELLIE: Look, my story is on the connection between this new incident and—

LOU: There isn't any connection.

ELLIE: It's practically the same story! Young black couple, decent, hard-working, buy a tiny little house in redneck territory—

LOU: If it's the same story, why write it?

ELLIE: Things have improved around here, partly due to your efforts. Schools desegregated twenty years ago—

LOU: And now we've got five-year-olds riding the bus an hour and a half each way. Black five-year-olds.

ELLIE: I heard you've gotten cynical.

LOU: Not cynical. Just bored.

ELLIE: Bored with racism?

LOU: It died back for a while. Now it's sprung up again, strong and green as honeysuckle. You ever see honeysuckle?

ELLIE: Not to recognize.

LOU: You're not from around here. Honeysuckle dies back every winter—looks like a jungle of dry sticks; but in the spring, first rain, first warm sun, it's up and moving fast, slinging loops over everything in its path.

ELLIE: Mind if I smoke?

LOU: You're still smoking? (*ELLIE nods. LOU rummages for an ashtray, finally takes one from her collection of "Negro" knickknacks.*) Used to be I couldn't write a speech without lighting up.

ELLIE (*She holds up the ashtray*): You stub out your butts in this?

LOU: No.

ELLIE: Just for guests?

LOU: I quit.

ELLIE: Don't give me a lecture. I've given up everything else.

LOU: My lecturing days are over.

ELLIE *(Examining ashtray):* You got more stuff like this—?

LOU *(Gesturing):* Whole shelf full. Black boy jockey—used to have them, life-size, outside every pair of white gates. Goldilocks doll, reverses to mammy . . . Bank with a black boy fishing for pennies . . .

ELLIE *(Getting up to examine these artifacts):* If I mention these in my story . . .

LOU: Mention away. Just don't forget to put in the honeysuckle.

ELLIE: Meaning—?

LOU: Meaning what I do, and what I believe, is above ground, out in the open; but the honeysuckle grows in the dark, in the night, it takes over when nobody's noticing. Sit down, turn that machine back on.

ELLIE *(Putting the mammy doll back on the shelf):* Where do you get this stuff?

LOU: Every yard sale, every flea market. Lest we forget . . .

ELLIE *(Returning to the table):* Most people believe we've gotten past racial hate.

LOU: Do you believe that baby's going to be born alive and well?

ELLIE: I don't see what my personal—

LOU: The first time you leave home to go to work, and you hear that baby crying—you think that'll have no effect on your career? You'll hear that crying for the rest of your life. When he's in trouble, you'll know it's because you walked away with that cry in your ears.

ELLIE: This is incredible.

LOU: Turn that machine back on! You want to talk about this "incident," this old story that goes on and on and never changes. . . . What was it that white woman said, out in Shiveley—?

ELLIE: You have been reading the newspaper.

LOU: TV. It slips in my eyes and ears. That woman in Shiveley —she's one step up from the trailer park, one step up from living as bad as the black people live here in the West End. "Shiveley's a good neighborhood," she told that TV lady. "Now this thing is going to ruin our reputation." She worked hard to buy that little house, scrounged for the down payment. That house is all she'll ever have, except for her children—and if she has any sense, she knows she doesn't have them! And now you have the gall to tell her she has to accept the kind of change she's never in her life accepted—black neighbors. The end of her hopes, the downfall of her dream. Every house on her block for sale, and nobody buying.

ELLIE: They're not going to believe this—

LOU: Yes, they will, because it's not true, and it's the not-true that makes the best story. When's that baby due?

ELLIE: Five and a half weeks. Would you say, Mrs. Alden, a white resident's rights, out there in Shiveley—

LOU: Tell you what, I'll come and see you in the hospital when that baby's two or three days old, and I'll tell you I've got a scoop for you, a real insider's story, absolutely exclusive, and you'll look at me like I'm crazy. You'll want to tell me how bad it hurt, how long it lasted, what the doctor said, what your husband said when he finally got there—

ELLIE: He's going to the delivery—

LOU: And then you'll want me to look at that miserable scrap of humanity, a nurse holding it up and smiling like she made it herself.

ELLIE *(Rising):* I guess I've done all I can here, Mrs. Alden.

LOU: Here! Turn this thing off! *(ELLIE does so.)* You go back down to the newspaper, tell them I'm a crazy old lady, doesn't even make sense anymore, gone back on everything I believed.

ELLIE: It was your daughter's death, wasn't it?
    (Pause)

LOU: Is that what they say?

ELLIE *(Holding out her hand):* Goodbye. I'm sorry—
LOU *(Brushing aside her hand):* I'm not. I don't like your questions. *(As ELLIE exits)* Let me know when you drop the kid! I'll come down to the hospital with that exclusive. . . .

Shamanism in New Jersey

ROSE CARUSO

The living room of a suburban house. Dawn. Lights rise to reveal ALONA sprawled on an old, clean armchair in a darkened living room. She is a young woman, half Native American and half Bloomfield, NJ. Dressed in white, her face thick with "ceremonial" makeup, her only movements are the slow, rhythmic chewing of gum and the constant clicking of the remote control with one outstretched hand. The flickering blue light from the television heightens the strange and somewhat disconcerting effect of this image. Is she a witch, a priestess of a primitive society, or a New Jersey counter girl?

After a moment, her mother, PHYLLIS, a model of convention, opens the door and stands in the doorway.

PHYLLIS: I thought I heard you in here. *(She clicks on a table lamp.)* Why are you sitting in the dark? How come you didn't turn the light on? *(Pause. PHYLLIS takes her in.)* Oh, no. What happened this time?

ALONA: Stop it, Ma.

PHYLLIS: What'd you do?

ALONA: I didn't do nothing. I told him. I told him it takes two girls to lift a tray of crumb buns. Not even just crumb buns. Anything. Two girls, I said. 'Cause you can't see where you're going when you're holding the tray and going from the back to the front. But, it's like he's an animal. He don't listen. He's just got that hair coming out of his neck with the sweat and flour, and those eyes—always looking like he wants to find you with your foot in a trap.

24

PHYLLIS: So what do you care what his eyes look like? *(PHYLLIS turns off the television.)*

ALONA: He's just like that asshole at the Nevada Diner. Always put me in a very Route 46 head. And then he tells me in front of Tara and Jeanette. He tells me in front of them, he says, if I come back and apologize to him, then maybe . . . MAYBE, he'll let me have my job back. Asshole.

PHYLLIS: Now every time I go there for bread, I have to be embarrassed. *(ALONA gets up and readies herself to leave.)* So, apologize. It isn't going to kill you. *(PHYLLIS stands at the window, her back to ALONA.)* Lemme get out of here. I have to return those wine glasses. *(To herself)* I don't know why I can't find a wine glass I like. It smells like coffee outside again. How come every time I get my hair done, it rains? You know, Alona, you take things too much to heart. Half the time, people don't even mean what they say. Not in New Jersey, anyway. Like when I'm driving, people are always yelling things at me and doing that thing with their finger. Do I think they mean it? Do I take those names and those things they do with their hands to heart? *(To herself)* It's like living by myself. I talk, and nobody answers. I'm going over to Tessie's for a while to finish things up. Every year, it's the same story. Everybody says they're going to help, and me and Tessie wind up doing all the cooking. Poor Tessie, this whole thing with Betty Lynn is making her so sick that the doctor put her on drugs, too. I think those little blue pills though are making her worse. *(PHYLLIS turns and sees ALONA ready to go out.)*

ALONA: Did you give Betty Lynn the comfrey tea I gave you?

PHYLLIS: What do you want to get involved for?

ALONA: You didn't give it to her.

PHYLLIS: Besides, you should be worrying about getting yourself together before you try helping someone else. So what are we doing here? You going to work?

ALONA: I don't know.

PHYLLIS: Go. He probably won't even remember saying it.

ALONA: It ain't him that's the problem.

PHYLLIS: Hurry up, you'll be late.

ALONA: I don't know, Ma. I said, I don't know.

PHYLLIS: Do what you want. But, if you don't go to work, I want you to get those weeds out of the kitchen. *Today.* You hear me?

ALONA: Herbs. Herbs, Ma. They're not weeds, they're herbs. Elder blossoms for fever, daisies and yarrow for wounds, and spice bush from the swamps of Secaucus.

PHYLLIS: Weeds . . . Herbs. All I know is they're making my kitchen smell strange. Elder blossom. What the hell is an elder blossom anyway?

ALONA: I explained.

PHYLLIS: Then explain again. Every time you explain, that's another time I don't understand. *(To herself)* Weeds hanging all over . . . Under the eaves of my house. Wild, strange smells coming out from everywhere. If you spent as much time thinking about how to talk to your boss as picking those weeds . . . ALONA, ARE YOU LISTENING TO ME? *(She softens.)* What's the matter, Alona? What happened? Things were going along so nicely at this job. You seemed . . . I don't know, not happy, but involved. That's it—involved. It was such a thrill for me to see the girls from the bakery calling, coming over . . . *(ALONA sits on the couch.)*

ALONA: I know. I'm sorry.

PHYLLIS: Why are you doing this to me?

ALONA: It's got nothing to do with you.

(PHYLLIS sits on the couch next to ALONA.)

PHYLLIS: When you were a little baby I used to hold your foot in my hand. I used to sleep next to you with your foot in my hand and your heart would beat in your foot. I never thought, laying next to you, with your beating foot in my hand. *(PHYLLIS looks at ALONA's hair.)* I never thought, holding your foot in my hand. I never thought that someday I'd see you walking out the door with your hair all teased up on top of your head like that.

(ALONA holds out her hand for money.)

ALONA: Ma. Spot me for a ten for gas.

PHYLLIS: No. 'Cause if I give it to you, you won't go. I know you.

ALONA: Ma.

PHYLLIS: No.

ALONA: Please.

PHYLLIS: No.

(ALONA goes to the door and opens it. She turns to her mother.)

ALONA: You know when you were feeling my heart in my foot, I never imagined that one day that foot would grow up and my own mother would keep it off the pedal of my Beretta. I couldn't even imagine it. *(ALONA walks out.)*

Stargazing

NANCY S. CHU

Two women in their mid to late twenties are in the waiting room of a doctor's office. GILLIAN is here to confirm her pregnancy and to consider an abortion, while JEANINE, a young mother and her soon-to-be sister-in-law, is here to offer her support. The two women do not have the best relationship, but have known each other for several years. Neither of their significant others (who happen to be brothers) knows about this visit to the doctor's office, and that they do agree on. GILLIAN is pacing in the space, while JEANINE sits in an uncomfortable chair, trying to concentrate on a newspaper. GILLIAN's pacing wears on JEANINE, who indicates the empty chair next to her. GILLIAN reluctantly sits and begins to read over JEANINE's shoulder. JEANINE offers her the paper and reaches for another one for herself. The women perform some synchronized movement with the newspaper. Finally, impatient, GILLIAN lowers her paper.

GILLIAN: How long have we been waiting here?

JEANINE *(Paper comes down, checks watch):* Forty minutes.
    (Both women eye the NURSE, who shifts in her seat. The papers come back up, hiding the women from the audience.)

GILLIAN *(Pulling the paper down slowly, peeking over the top):* I didn't expect so many people here. *(They look at the audience, the "others.")* I guess I'm not the only person in town with problems. *(GILLIAN's paper goes up, as JEANINE's comes down.)*

JEANINE: No, you never are. *(JEANINE's paper goes up, while GILLIAN's comes down. She looks at JEANINE, puzzled. She slowly returns to her paper. After a pause, JEANINE folds her paper and confronts GILLIAN.)* Does Brady know you're here?

GILLIAN *(Quickly folding her paper and dropping it on the floor):* No. He thinks I've gone shopping. Oh, that reminds me, I have to get milk, eggs, and chocolate ice cream before I go home. Maybe I'll make ham marsala for dinner tonight. . . . I haven't made that in a while. . . . Brady likes that. You know, I should make a list. I usually do, but . . . I haven't been really thinking clearly lately. . . .

(GILLIAN *trails off and mumbles about dinner. She fumbles in her bag for a pen and paper.* JEANINE *takes it from her and sets it down.*)

JEANINE: Stop . . . hey, listen, there's nothing to be nervous about. Just relax.

GILLIAN: I can't relax.

(GILLIAN *moves into a spot.* JEANINE *freezes behind her newspaper.*)

Any second now I'm going to go behind that door, where a nurse practitioner is going to set me up on a table, strap my feet into stirrups, and I will have to endure cold metal penetrating between my legs. (JEANINE *turns a page of the paper and crosses her legs.*) She will peer into my womb, scrape my insides with a cotton swab, and press down on my belly, asking me in a sweet, yet condescending tone, "Does that hurt? Am I pressing too hard?" And I will have to say, "No, it's fine." But it's not fine. I'm not fine. I'm scared shitless, and furious with myself for letting this happen. I'm furious that Jeanine has to sit here next to me, because I am afraid to tell Brady . . . although I will be eternally grateful that she is here. Why can't I tell Brady, I ask myself, the other half of this mess . . . the reason why I'm here in the first place? I don't know. I know he wouldn't abandon me; he's not like that. But I guess I'm afraid that he simply wouldn't know what to say, and I don't know if I could love him anymore after that moment. I know that wouldn't be fair. . . . I mean, what could he possibly say that wouldn't make me resent him right now?

(GILLIAN *returns to her seat and both resume waiting.*)

JEANINE: You know, don't take this the wrong way, but this happens all the time. I mean, just look at the number of people in here right now (*Indicating the audience*). You'll be fine. No matter how things end up, whether they seem for the best or for the worst, you just pick yourself up and keep living your life. Things may change, but I think at some point, you realize that everything happens for the best . . . *(More to herself)* or at least you make yourself believe that. And that's OK, too, I think, if that's what you need to do.

GILLIAN: How could you say that to me? How can you expect me to accept that?

JEANINE: I'm not saying you have to accept it, I'm just trying to tell you that a lot of—

GILLIAN: Why are you trying to tell me how to think? What gives you the right? How the hell would you know what it feels like to be me right now? You sit there with your perfect family and your wonderful life—

JEANINE: Are you sure you want to say that? You don't know—

GILLIAN: I know Robert loves you, and you love him. I know that Hannah is the most wonderful thing in your life. I know you and Robert share everything—

JEANINE: Do we?

GILLIAN: —with each other, and Brady and I . . . I can't even tell him the truth because I'm afraid he might just not want—

JEANINE *(Interrupting):* They're calling you.

GILLIAN *(Somewhat dazed, looking around):* Wha—

JEANINE: The nurse is calling you. Are you sure you don't want me to come in?

GILLIAN *(Gathering her senses and bags):* No, I'm fine, stay here, please, I need to do this alone. . . . *(Pause, regrets her words)* Listen, I'm sorry. I didn't mean that, I just . . . *(Searching for words)*

JEANINE *(Smiling):* She's waiting. *(GILLIAN smiles back weakly, turns and exits. JEANINE follows her to the door, then turns to sit.)* This is a tough time for her . . . believe me, I know. I can't be angry at her for getting upset with me. After all, Robert and I never told anyone that we got married because of Hannah. We were planning on staying out west, but then . . . *(Gestures vaguely at stomach)* and then he decided to come home to take over his dad's business instead. . . . Nobody ever knew. We came home married and expecting. When you're in that situation, you can't see beyond the pain and the fear, and you lash out, hoping the people who really love you will forgive you afterwards. Sometimes I wonder if Robert has ever forgiven me, or if I've forgiven him. When I look back at my life, I realize that Hannah is the most beautiful thing to have ever happened to me. She is so perfect, this little human being that two people created, who breathes and cries and smiles. . . . I can't remember what life was like before she was born. And yet, sometimes I look at her and I see the reason why Robert no longer laughs or touches me the way he used to, and I realize that I don't even want him to anymore. . . . Sometimes I see that in Hannah, and I hate myself for resenting her, for resenting the one person who had the least amount of choice in the whole matter. *(Realizing she has shared too much, JEANINE sits down, and takes the rest of the monologue to herself.)* When we found out I was pregnant, Robert and I made a choice. He really was quite the man to take full responsibility . . . and I loved him anyway. Waiting for Hannah . . . the excitement, really held us together.

(GILLIAN enters and stands at the door watching JEANINE.)
But now, it's very hard, hard to remember the love behind that decision when she cries at 3:00 in the morning, and someone has to get up to feed her, or the doctor's bills come in and we don't quite have the money to pay. Sometimes, I look in Robert's eyes and I see him so far away from us—I know he wonders what life would have been like if we had just . . .

GILLIAN *(Interrupting):* Jeanine?

JEANINE *(Sees GILLIAN, but decides to finish thought):* But then I stop myself. I can't afford to think like that. Not at this point. And I really do think things have worked out for the best. I suppose I need to believe that right now. *(Turns to GILLIAN)* Well?

GILLIAN: Six weeks. I have two more to decide.
    (They let the information sink in.)

JEANINE: Oh. I was really hoping—

GILLIAN: Yeah, so was I.

JEANINE *(Changing the topic and offering GILLIAN her bag):* So . . . eggs, milk, ice cream . . .

GILLIAN *(Taking the bag):* And ham . . .

(They start to leave.)

JEANINE: I still haven't thought about what I'm going to make tonight yet . . . maybe I'll make ham marsala, too . . .

(They ad-lib about dinner as they exit.)

Composing Tchaikovsky

LAURA EDMONDSON

The play tells the story of two women in Tchaikovsky's life: NADEZHDA, his benefactress, with whom he exchanged numerous letters but whom he never met, and ANTONINA, with whom he had a brief and disastrous marriage. ANTONINA speaks from an asylum to which she was consigned for many years until her death, while NADEZHDA speaks from her bedroom in her Moscow mansion, where she secludes herself from society. ANTO-NINA is looking into a mirror, primping, and NADEZHDA is fussing with her photographs. As the lights come up fully, ANTONINA glances at the audience. ('/' indicates where speeches overlap.)

ANTONINA: Oh, dear. They're early.

NADEZHDA: No, they aren't. They're just being prompt. *(Smiles at audience)* I admire promptness. Speaks well of your upbringing.

ANTONINA: Means they got nothing better / to do—

NADEZHDA *(A warning):* Antonina . . .

ANTONINA: except come and gawk at the poor creatures in the asylum.

NADEZHDA *(Hastily, to audience): She's* the one in an asylum, not me.

ANTONINA: But the boundary is so easily crossed . . . *(To audience)* Would you like to know why they put me here?/ Hmm?

NADEZHDA: Antonina!

ANTONINA: What?

NADEZHDA: Must you tell them that so soon? You'll scare them off.

ANTONINA: Look at them. They're dying to know.

NADEZHDA *(To audience):* Don't encourage her.

ANTONINA *(To audience):* I've been locked away for five years, a danger to you all.

NADEZHDA *(Briskly):* Did they give you your bath?

ANTONINA: Oh yes. I smell like a rose. Would you like to smell me, Nadezhda dear? To make sure I'm fit for our company.

NADEZHDA: No thank you.

ANTONINA: Your loss. *(To audience)* Would any of you like to smell me? Taste me,/ perhaps?

NADEZHDA *(Overlapping, hastily):* Allow me to introduce myself. I'm Nadezhda. Nadezhda Fileratovna von Meck!
(NADEZHDA looks at the audience expectantly.)

ANTONINA: Doesn't mean a thing to them, old girl.

NADEZHDA: Humph. By the end of tonight, it will. *(To audience)* I could repeat it for you, if you like.

ANTONINA: My name, now . . . *that* is a name they will recognize, a name that will make them lean forward in hopes of touching my skirt—looking up my skirt—as I saunter by . . .
(Audience shows no interest.)

NADEZHDA: They're not here to see you.

ANTONINA: Well. Neither are they here for you.

NADEZHDA: I know. They want him.

ANTONINA *(Bitterly):* What a surprise.

NADEZHDA: Oh, Antonina. Who can blame them? I'm sure I'd feel the same way. *(Smiles graciously at audience)* I understand. And you shall have him—that is, you shall hear his music, which is practically the same thing.

ANTONINA: No. No music!

NADEZHDA: They're guests, Antonina. Their wishes come first. *(To audience)* I have hired my very own orchestra, to obey my every wish. And yours.

ANTONINA: What about mine?

NADEZHDA: Just a symphony, perhaps two, and then we can start again.

ANTONINA *(To audience):* This is your fault. She's giving up because you didn't recognize her name.

NADEZHDA: Conductor! I'm ready! *(To audience)* What would you like to hear? Of course, anything by my darling Peter—

ANTONINA: That bastard—

NADEZHDA: is simply sheer delight!

(The opening chords of The Fourth Symphony *ring out over the audience. Lights begin to dim on ANTONINA and NADEZHDA, but stop when ANTONINA shouts over the music.)*

ANTONINA: STOP IT!

(Music stops abruptly.)

NADEZHDA: How dare you!

ANTONINA: At least let me introduce myself first. That's all I ask. *(NADEZHDA just glares at her. ANTONINA turns to the audience. She is anxious, but trying not to show it.)* Good evening. My name is Antonina Ivanovna Tchaikovskaia. The lovely—

NADEZHDA: deranged—

ANTONINA: long-forgotten wife of Peter Illyich Tchaikovsky—

NADEZHDA: one of the most brilliant—

ANTONINA: overrated—

NADEZHDA: composers that the world will ever know. *(NADEZHDA steps forward.)* And I am Nadezhda von Meck— the greatest friend that *Peter* has ever known.

(Pause)

Well. That should do it.

ANTONINA: Nadezhda, we've only just begun.

(The Fourth Symphony resumes softly in the background. Pause while the music plays.)

ANTONINA *(To audience):* I've been watching you. You were only pretending to listen to the music. . . . You're much more interested in looking at me. Oh, now. Don't deny it, my darlings.

NADEZHDA: Don't insult them. Of course they were listening— how could they ignore such beauty?

ANTONINA *(Preening):* That's what I meant.

NADEZHDA *(Ignoring her, to audience):* This is *The Fourth Symphony* . . . *our* symphony . . . that's what Peter always calls it—our symphony, dedicated to me, to Nadezhda von

Meck—to his best friend. *(She pauses, savoring the moment. Music fades.)* Whenever he plays it, he thinks of me, aching to rush home and write me a letter. One of his dear, sweet letters that brings joy to my old heart.

ANTONINA: Here she goes. Her silly letters . . .

NADEZHDA: One day, my dear, they will make my name. *(NADEZHDA kneels by the leather trunk. To audience)* This trunk contains all the letters he's written me over the years. . . . So far, we have exchanged over a thousand. *(She opens the trunk with reverence.)* And such letters! I can pick any one of these, at delicious random, and be instantly assured of his love, his deep abiding love for Nadezhda Fileratovna.

ANTONINA *(To audience):* Notice how she keeps repeating her name for you.

NADEZHDA: Ah. Listen to this one. "Dearest Nadezhda. A famous actor once said that he always picks out one sympathetic face in the audience and plays for that person. I will take his advice, and compose only for you." *(Blushing with delight)* Oh, isn't he a dear?

ANTONINA *(To audience):* Remember he's writing to the woman who sends him 6,000 rubles a year.

NADEZHDA: A pittance. A mere pittance!

ANTONINA: Perhaps to you, Madame Owner of a Railroad.

NADEZHDA: Or this one. "My matchless Nadezhda! You are the only person in the world who can make me happy, profoundly happy. I can only hope that whatever inspires your feeling for me—"

ANTONINA: and your annual allowance—

NADEZHDA: "—will never end nor alter, because such a loss I could not endure." *(NADEZHDA gazes at the letter for a moment, then abruptly crumples it in her hand.)*

ANTONINA *(Innocently):* How long has it been since he's written? *(NADEZHDA lowers her head and focuses on smoothing out the letter.)*

NADEZHDA *(Brightly):* Not long. Not long at all. He keeps so busy now—why, he just got back from America.

ANTONINA: Did he enjoy it?

NADEZHDA: A letter will come from him today, telling me all about it!

ANTONINA: Dr. Korsakov tells me that the Americans still chain madwomen to the walls.

NADEZHDA: How barbaric! You're lucky to be a Russian, Antonina.

ANTONINA *(Sardonic):* As lucky as they come.

NADEZHDA *(Reconsidering):* Yes, well—

ANTONINA: Luckier than you, at any rate.

NADEZHDA: I beg your pardon?

ANTONINA: We're both wasting away—but *my* wasting away will be remembered.

(NADEZHDA laughs.)

NADEZHDA: My poor deluded girl.

ANTONINA: The pathetic but oh-so-attractive madwoman is far more appealing than the pathetic but *not*-so-attractive old widow.

(NADEZHDA has pulled out another letter.)

NADEZHDA: Listen to this one. "Whatever may happen, I never want to see Antonina Ivanovna for the rest of my life! I wish her every happiness, which does not prevent me from hating her *deeply.* I have never met a more *unpleasant* human being. She is *hateful* to me, *hateful* to the point of insanity."

(NADEZHDA looks at ANTONINA with a "so there" expression.)

ANTONINA *(Cheerful):* My husband always had a way with words.

NADEZHDA: This is how you'll be remembered, Antonina. As a . . .

ANTONINA: A bitch?

NADEZHDA: Well, yes.

ANTONINA: And a whore.

NADEZHDA: That too.

ANTONINA: I can die happy then.

NADEZHDA: That doesn't bother you?

ANTONINA: No.

NADEZHDA *(Suspicious):* Why not?

ANTONINA: Let's just say I've used my time here wisely. *(ANTO-NINA produces a stack of papers from underneath her mattress.)*

NADEZHDA: And what is that?

ANTONINA *(Fondly):* My memoirs.

NADEZHDA: Your what?

ANTONINA: *My Life with Tchaikovsky,* by Antonina Ivanovna Tchaikovskaia. I considered *My Life with That Bastard,* but I'm going for that sweet and innocent tone.

NADEZHDA: How . . . interesting.

ANTONINA: More than interesting. It's going to make those letters of yours look like stewed potatoes. *(She looks at her memoirs with the same reverence NADEZHDA gives to her letters.)* A red cover, I think. A red leather cover, my name embossed in gold . . .

NADEZHDA: What are you saying about him?

  (ANTONINA laughs.)

ANTONINA: Wouldn't you like to know!

NADEZHDA: You're . . . not—

ANTONINA: Yes?

NADEZHDA: Antonina!

ANTONINA *(Innocently):* Why, is something wrong?

NADEZHDA: You can't tell everything!

ANTONINA: Why not?

NADEZHDA: It would destroy him.

ANTONINA: I could use the company.

NADEZHDA: But—he's at the height of his success now, his music is better than ever—

ANTONINA: A little pain is good for art.

NADEZHDA: I won't allow it. I'll have them suppressed.

ANTONINA: I'm going to outlive you by a good many years, old girl. I will publish them. I will make *my* name.

  (Pause)

NADEZHDA: If you can even find a publisher. You have a pathetic way with words.

ANTONINA: How do you know?

NADEZHDA: He's quoted parts of your letters to me—

ANTONINA: Those letters were private!

NADEZHDA: "My darling Petya, I cannot live without you and that's why I shall do away with myself." Drivel. Complete *lovesick* drivel . . . I shudder at the thought of fifty pages of it.

ANTONINA: More like three hundred.

NADEZHDA: A waste of good paper.

ANTONINA: Publishers will be clawing at my door.

NADEZHDA: They'll be vomiting on the pages.

ANTONINA: You don't know what you're talking about!

(Pause)

NADEZHDA: Read some of it to me, then.

ANTONINA: No.

(They eye each other with distrust.)

You wouldn't be able to handle it. What Peter was really like.

NADEZHDA: I know him far better than you.

ANTONINA: The music is not the man. I have known the man, and I have put him *here. (She stabs a finger at the memoirs. To audience)* I'll read some of my memoirs to you when *she's* not around. That's a promise.

NADEZHDA: How about some more music?

ANTONINA: Not again!

NADEZHDA: Yes, I think his violin concerto would be just about right. The *Cazonetta.*

(The Violin Concerto begins to play.)

ANTONINA: I can't believe this.

NADEZHDA *(To audience):* One of the many remarkable things about Peter's music is that it permits you to escape . . . transcend . . . the moment. Ahh.

ANTONINA: I hate this song.

NADEZHDA: It's a concerto, *dear,* not a song. *(To audience)* Full of poetic dreaming and secret desires. I wrote him after I heard it. And sadness. Sadness for what could have been, and never was . . .

(ANTONINA watches NADEZHDA lose herself in the music and—reluctantly—turns her gaze to the imaginary orchestra and begins to listen herself. Music and lights fade.)

Marla's Devotion

LINDA EISENSTEIN

MARLA and JOEY's living room. MARLA, a perennial student, and her partner JOEY, an attorney, are getting ready in the morning. MARLA is doing a prostrating meditation. She takes a deep breath—takes two steps forward—breathes—then bends, kneels, and lies down prostrate, facedown, her arms stretched forward. She then rises and takes two more steps, lies down, prostrate, etc. She rather resembles an inchworm. JOEY is bustling around, drinking coffee, getting her briefcase ready for work.

JOEY: Zoom, zoom, zoom. Time to get cracking.

MARLA: What time do you want dinner?

JOEY: Dinner is doubtful. Depositions most of the day, then court. That means the drive-through and the law library tonight.

MARLA: Oh. Which case is it? The slimebag one?

JOEY: That doesn't narrow it down, Marla. OK, you remember the one, she was ironing the prick bastard's shirts, and the prick bastard took the iron and—

MARLA *(Hands over her ears):* Oooh, stop, no more! *(Takes a big breath, makes the next prostration an especially mindful one.)*

JOEY: Yes, my practice is such a jolly picnic lately. Also I gotta file a couple more restraining orders and . . . *(Finally noticing what MARLA is doing)* What's that, yoga?

MARLA: Kind of.

JOEY: That's the same one you were doing before my shower. Shouldn't you move on to a different exercise?

MARLA: It's something I'm trying out. From that article I was reading? These two monks did this as a devotion, Every two steps, they'd kneel down and do a full prostration.

JOEY: What the hell did they do that for?

MARLA: The article didn't say. For mindfulness, I guess. They walked between two temples in California like this.

JOEY: Jeez. I'll bet their knees were sore. Goodbye kiss. *(JOEY leans down to MARLA. They peck their morning goodbye.)*

MARLA *(Arms around JOEY's neck, trying to hold her):* Joey—

JOEY: Gotta run, babe.

MARLA: You're working late an awful lot lately.

JOEY *(Pulling away):* Can't be helped right now.

MARLA: I hardly see you.

JOEY: It's wacko season, OK? Hey, do me a favor. Stop by the cleaners on your way to class, all right?

MARLA: I . . . I don't think I'm going.

JOEY: Marla, don't cut class again.

MARLA: What's the point, anyway?

JOEY: Marla, it's simple. You go to class, you actually complete your assignments and turn them in, and eventually they hand you a diploma.

MARLA: Well, I'll go tomorrow. Right now I need to get the hang of this.

JOEY: The hang of what?

MARLA: This. This practice. It's really fascinating.

JOEY: Aw Jeez.

MARLA: I feel like I need to get more mindfulness and devotion in my life.

JOEY: You need to get more completed credit hours into your life so you can fucking *graduate.*

MARLA: You don't have to yell. *(MARLA does deep breathing through JOEY's mini-rant, trying to tune it out. The following overlaps a lot.)*

JOEY: I'm not yelling. You and that goddamn magazine. I dread, I absolutely dread the day it comes.

MARLA: You're so angry all the time.

JOEY: You always start in with some kind of *thing,*

MARLA: At the drop of a hat, you yell, Joey.

JOEY: some kind of hapless New Age bullshit.

MARLA: Buddhism isn't exactly New Age.

JOEY: I have to tell you that the very idea of this pisses me off.

MARLA: It's only, like, 3000 years old or something.

JOEY: Pardon me for saying so, Marla, but you of all people do *not* need more contact with a religious ideology that says your ego identity is an illusion.

MARLA: Like you know anything about Buddhism.

JOEY: You think I haven't read your stupid magazine? There's never anything else to read in the john. That, or the Miracles of the Bootie-satvas.

MARLA: Bodhisattvas. *(*BO-DEE-SAHT-VAHS*)*

JOEY: Whatever.

MARLA: I think it's a beautiful concept. Compassionate egoless saints who resist giving themselves over to total bliss until all sentient beings in the world are enlightened.

JOEY: Yeah, yeah, yeah. Well, let me tell ya what I noticed about your Bootie-satvas, Marla. Most of 'em are men. And they all had a bunch of years soldiering and screwing and carrying on before they saw the light and got all holy. That's what women need. Spend some time building up their ego's muscles, creating some havoc and a good fight. Then they can let go of it. Otherwise what you got is just another doormat for the Patriarchy.

MARLA: I don't think you get it, Joey.

JOEY: Now maybe this groveling on the ground *would* be good for monks.

MARLA: Life does not have to be a war.

JOEY: *Male* monks.

MARLA: This helps you breathe easier.

JOEY: But getting down on your knees every 30 seconds? I think this is a really fucked-up thing for a lesbian to be doing.

MARLA: It concentrates the mind, too.

JOEY: This is a bid for attention, that's what it is.

MARLA: No it's not.

JOEY: For my attention. Christ, you've already made me late.

MARLA: So go to work, Joey.

JOEY: A struggle for control. This, this is a very male thing you're doing.

MARLA: So what. If I were struggling for control in a female way I would eat and throw up. I prefer this. *(She breathes.)* It's rather peaceful when you inhale before the two steps, then exhale as you go prone. *(She goes prone.)* Actually, I think I'll stay down here for a while.

JOEY: Honest to God, Marla, I really cannot have you doing this to my life all the time. I have to get to work!

MARLA: Go right ahead. This isn't about you, anyway.

JOEY: Oh, sure.

MARLA: This is about me.

JOEY: You know, you're going to be in a world of hurt soon. Wait'll you have to get to the bathroom.

MARLA: I'll just have to plan ahead. No one said you have to get very far. It took those monks two and a half years to go fifty miles.

JOEY: When you get the runs? Don't say I didn't warn you. *(She exits.)*

(Lights down to a spot on MARLA.)

MARLA: Joey never exactly says it, but she thinks of me as a dilettante. This is how she sees it. She's the goal-directed one, and I'm the one who floats around, being arty. Just because it's taken me a while longer to get through school. But I do have goals. They're just not the kind of goals she recognizes.

Right now my goal is to pay attention to the workings of my own mind. This seems like a good way to stay alert to it. I take two steps forward, and then I kneel down and prostrate myself, and then I get back up, all the time being absolutely mindful of what I'm doing and thinking.

You know one of the first things I noticed? How utterly distracted I am. How scattered. How many times a day I find myself staring off in space, my mind floating in fantasy. Or how I can find myself standing in front of the refrigerator with the door open, staring inside. Like some new delight is going to miraculously appear in there. And I pace around so much, I can put down my coffee cup and then not be able to find it without wandering in circles from room to room.

Not any more. Now I have to really *want* that cup of coffee. I can't just spring up and get it on a whim. If I want to read a book, or eat a piece of cake, or answer the phone— well, I have to set my priorities. All the time being aware. I think being aware is a darn good goal!

Joey was right about one thing, though. When you're doing this? Diarrhea is no picnic.

(Blackout. Lights up on MARLA sitting down, reading. It is late. She has her legs elevated on a little pillow. JOEY comes in.)

JOEY *(Reacting to something offstage as she enters):* Ay, shut up, already! *(To MARLA)* Tell me—does the guy *ever* say one nice word to his dog? Or does he just scream at it all day long?

MARLA: How was court?

JOEY: Unbelievable. Horrible. Grotesque. Sociopathic maniacs loose upon society. And that's my colleagues. The clients are merely pathetic.

MARLA: Hello kiss. *(JOEY bends down for their little peck.)* You're kind of late.

JOEY: Tell me about it. I could die right here. What's with the pillows? *(Squeezes one of MARLA's knees.)*

MARLA: OW!!

JOEY: Whoa, sorry.

MARLA: My legs are a little sore, that's all. Want some dinner?

JOEY: No, no, babe, don't get up, I'm not really hungry.

(Nevertheless, JOEY sits down and MARLA gets up. JOEY begins to read the paper, not looking up until indicated.)

MARLA: Well, I had a pretty interesting day.

JOEY: Uh-huh. Where's the Metro section?

(As MARLA begins to move around the apartment, getting food ready, she does her prostrations. It's very hard for her to keep her mind on speaking, walking, prostrating, and putting together chips and salsa on a tray—so there are many stops and starts, jerks and halts and doubling back. JOEY mostly ad-libs

grunts and uh-huhs and sputters about things in the paper, but doesn't notice what MARLA is doing until indicated.)

MARLA: I learned a lot about myself today. You wouldn't believe it, Joey. I don't think I've ever had a day like this. I never even left the house. It was unbelievably stimulating, just walking around—well, kind of walking around—just *being* in here. I mean, here in my head! My mind was just, zap, zoom, boom. Insights! God, such insights! And . . . shoot, where'd I put . . . oh, there's the salsa. And in the middle of all of this, this incredible gestalt, my mom called. And I didn't have even one panic attack, not one!

JOEY: Arlene? What'd she want?

MARLA: Who knows? She was beating around the bush, as usual. Something about tulip time, and a bus trip to Holland.

JOEY: How the hell can you take a bus to Holland, that's Arlene for you all right.

MARLA: Holland, Michigan, it's a triple-A tour or something. But the point is, the point is! I just let her talk and I didn't freak out. I didn't have to analyze her every hidden motive. I couldn't actually, I was too busy trying to breathe and straighten my legs. It was amazing!

(By now, MARLA has the tray of chips and salsa and is wending her way over to JOEY. But she can't figure out how to carry it and do prostrations at the same time, so she has to keep putting down the tray and picking it up.)

JOEY *(Finally looking):* Marla—what the hell are you doing?

MARLA: I'm bringing you your chips and salsa. With no help from you, thanks a heap.

JOEY: Not that—Jeez, are you still . . . Look at you.

MARLA: Have you been listening to me? This is what I've been telling you about. Doing my prostrations. *(JOEY listens, incredulous.)* They're incredible. Amazing. Absolutely life-changing. My knees kind of need an ice pack, though.

JOEY: Well, sit down, then, ya goofball.

MARLA: Thank you, I think I will. *(Plops down.)*

JOEY: You've actually been doing this all day.

MARLA: Mm-hm.

JOEY: All day. And you didn't stop once.

MARLA: Unh-unh. Well, I forgot for a couple of minutes when the phone rang, and I started pacing around out of habit, but—I went right back to it.

JOEY *(With some admiration, in spite of herself):* That's amazing.

MARLA: Oh, and now and then I'd catch myself staring soulfully into the refrigerator. But even so, boom, right back.

JOEY: That is quite a feat of concentration. I mean, especially for you.

MARLA: It was pretty astounding, yeah.

JOEY: I don't quite know what to say. I don't think I've ever seen you actually focus on anything—quite like that.

MARLA: I surprised myself, actually.

JOEY: Well, you have had quite a day.

MARLA: Yup.

JOEY: What . . . what actually prompted this?

MARLA: Well, it was partly the Tarot card reading.

JOEY: Oh. Naturally.

(JOEY listens—mixed amusement, fascination, dismay—a very Lucy-and-Ricky moment—then a sneaking realization.)

MARLA: See, I did my cards again, and the Queen came up, the one with the pineapple wand, the one I can't stand because she means "go on a diet"? Well, there she was again, and the Prince of Disks too, the guy who stands for more exercise, and I get these two all the time, one or the other, and usually I hate them? But I got *both*, so this time I read the book more carefully, and I found out that the Pineapple Queen *really* means "taking in a diet of things that sustain you," and I realized it could mean thoughts, too, and the Prince with his chariot full of boulders *really* stood for "Building New Worlds" and removing obstacles in your life, not just ridiculous aerobics in ill-fitting leotards—and all of a sudden—I liked these cards! The pictures actually looked attractive and healthy and I thought of the new worlds I'd be building and it *was* an exercise, kind of, and all this

47

breathing in and breathing out was kind of, you know, a new way to nourish myself. So I decided it *was* good for me and I'd keep doing it.

(A long pause.)

JOEY *(Some relief):* Is THAT what this is about? Your weight again? Marla, honey, how many times do I have to say it? I like the way you look. Really.

MARLA: It isn't that.

JOEY: Sure it is. You think I'm going to run off with some skinny butt girl, is that it?

MARLA: No-o. *(She means maybe.)* Although you were paying an awful lot of attention to that Pam person at the PRIDE rally.

JOEY: I was surprised to see her, that's all, she works for the Clerk of Courts! I was just . . . a little startled.

MARLA: Well, she was startling, all right, in those size-4 short-shorts and open-toed shoes, and hot pink nail polish on her toes, for crying out loud.

JOEY: I looked, OK. I admit I looked.

MARLA: She's tiny, and blonde, and cute.

JOEY: Yes she is. In a kind of trampy fluff-muffin sort of way, but honey, I mean, my God, she makes copies of *documents.* I love *you*, Marla.

MARLA: See, this is what I mean.

JOEY: I was just looking.

MARLA: My thoughts just fly around and around,

JOEY: And I have to be nice to her, or my motions will get lost in File Hell and never emerge.

MARLA: in all these grotesque ways and—that's my point! That's why I have to do this. Clear my mind every two steps. Otherwise it's all chattering monkeys, I have no control of my ridiculous thoughts.

(The following is tease, cuddle, and make up.)

JOEY: Thank you.

MARLA: I admit they're ridiculous.

JOEY: Thank you.

MARLA: And you're not trying to make it with big hair Pam.

JOEY: Her toes are shaped funny, too, did you see? They're crooked. Who could want a woman with crooked toes.

MARLA: Really.

JOEY: I like your toes.

MARLA: Thank you.

JOEY: Although at the moment, they're dangling at the end of knees that look a little swollen, to tell the truth.

MARLA: Yup.

JOEY: Well, we'll just have to get you off your feet.

MARLA: Sounds nice.

JOEY *(Beckoning toward their bedroom, offstage)*: Step into my office.

MARLA *(A little kiss)*: Okay.

JOEY: C'mon. Time for some real exercise. *(She goes offstage.)*
(MARLA begins to follow JOEY offstage, then remembers to stop herself after two steps—does her prostration. Gets up—prostrates—etc. She tries to hurry.)

MARLA: I'll be right there.

JOEY *(Coming back out)*: What's taking . . . oh my God.

MARLA: I said I'll be right there.

JOEY: You're crawling. You're actually crawling?!

MARLA: No I'm not, it's only a couple of prostrations from here to the bedroom.

JOEY: This is unbelievable, stop it!

MARLA: I have to be consistent with my practice, I don't—

JOEY: Your *practice?*

MARLA: I don't want to start making exceptions, not any, or pretty soon I won't do it at all.

JOEY: I thought this was an experiment!

MARLA: I know myself.

JOEY: Marla, I can't have you crawling into the . . . oh, man.

MARLA: Why not?

JOEY: It's . . . it's too damn kinky, that's why.

MARLA: Well, try to incorporate it into a turn-on.

JOEY: A turn-on? You look like a caterpillar inching up a leaf!!

MARLA: Well, I guess I'm just your little caterpillar then.

JOEY *(Bolting over to the other side of the room):* No, no, no—this is totally not OK.

MARLA: Joey, don't move around so much. It just makes it harder for me to get there.

JOEY: I am totally not in the mood. I mean, call me old-fashioned. But I don't want to play those dominance-submission games, they freak me out, OK?

MARLA: That's not what this is.

JOEY: OK, then. So stop.

MARLA: I can't, I told you . . .

JOEY: Oh, Jesus, this is a good one. This one is just a peach. "Dear Abby: I'm having a little problem with my sex life. My girlfriend insists on crawling on her hands and knees everywhere because the Pineapple Queen and the Prince of Exercise told her it was a good idea. What shall I do?"

MARLA: OK.

JOEY: Marla, are you trying to drive me insane?

MARLA: No.

JOEY: What have I done to you, tell me what have I done. I know I don't pay enough attention to you, but Christ, baby, you know what my practice is like these days!

MARLA: Yes, I know.

JOEY: All day long, phones ringing, women crying their eyes out,

MARLA: Your *practice.*

JOEY: in and out of my office with busted teeth and broken ribs, it's one horror show after another.

MARLA: Well, this is MY practice.

JOEY: When I come home all I want is a little peace. A little peace of mind. That's all I want.

MARLA *(Starting to cry):* That's all any of us wants, Joey. That's all I want. Peace of mind.

JOEY: Then why can't I have it, huh? Why can't I fucking have it?!?

   (JOEY storms out of the apartment. Door slams.)

MARLA: I don't know. I don't know. *(Crying, she tries to get control of her breathing, big breaths in and out — then a breathing chant.)*
Ah-ah-ah-hummmm. Ah-ah-ah-hummmm.
That's all anybody wants.
Ah-ah-ah-hummmm.
Peace of mind.
(Lights dim on MARLA *in the middle of the floor, breathing, centering.)*

Flappers

ANNIE EVANS

Lights rise on LUPIE, an ex-flapper, sitting in a wheelchair by a gramophone, which is playing an old 20s recording. ANDY, in her twenties, stands nearby with keys and her bag. She is here to be a companion for LUPIE while her niece/caretaker is on vacation.

ANDY: MRS. REED! MRS. REED! Great. YOU CAN'T KEEP DOING THIS ALL DAY.

LUPIE: HELL I CAN'T!

ANDY: YOU HAVE TO DEAL WITH ME, MRS. REED. Unbelievable. *(Looks about)* Jesus, look at this place. *(Back to LUPIE)* OK MRS. REED. TWO CAN PLAY THIS GAME.

(ANDY takes a Walkman and a large chemistry book out of her bag. She sits, puts on the headphones and starts to read. LUPIE becomes immediately furious. She takes off the needle, rolls over to ANDY, and pulls off her headphones.)

LUPIE: Stop that and get out.

ANDY: Not so nice, is it?

LUPIE: This is my house. I can be as rude as I please. Now leave before I call the police.

ANDY: Mrs. Reed—

LUPIE: And stop calling me that. My name is Lupie.

ANDY: Lupie?

LUPIE: It's always been Lupie. I only respond to Lupie.

ANDY: Fine, Lupie, I'm sorry I missed your niece, but the bus broke an axle outside Hartford. I know this is awkward. I called. She said in her note she told you I called, that I was on my way. You do . . . know who I am?

LUPIE: I haven't the slightest.

ANDY: . . .You're joking, right?

LUPIE: I'm being facetious. That's not joking. It's talking down to people. Which means I'm talking down to you. I hope you're offended and leave.

ANDY: I can't leave. You know that.

LUPIE: What—your feet only move in one direction?

ANDY: You need someone to stay here—

LUPIE: I have no intention of letting some stranger live under my roof and mess with my things while my prudish doctor niece tries to get air blown between her legs at some Club Mediterranean.

ANDY: This is hard enough as it is, Mrs. Ree— I mean, Lupie. Can't you be a little more cooperative?

LUPIE: Cooperative? I'm going to call the police about a trespasser. *(Rolls toward the telephone)*

ANDY: Lupie. This is ridiculous. Lupie. I'm not leaving. What if something happens? Lupie! Your niece already warned the precinct you might be calling. *(LUPIE stops rolling.)* Sorry, it's in the note. I guess she knows you pretty well.

LUPIE: I do not need a babysitter. It's insulting.

ANDY: I understand.

LUPIE: And I hate liars.

ANDY: You're right, I don't understand. I empathize.

LUPIE: Well, stop it. I have lived alone in this house for twenty years. I could have hired a circus to entertain me, but I did not.

ANDY: Yes, but you got sick, you need help.

LUPIE: I can take care of myself! Now will you please respect my wishes and leave me alone.

ANDY: I don't know what to say.

LUPIE: Say goodbye.

ANDY: It's a little too late for that. I'm here. I've nowhere else to stay.

LUPIE: I'll put you up in the Algonquin for the next twenty-one days.

ANDY: I can't do that.

LUPIE: The Plaza. Help the little old ladies in and out of the Oak Room and we'll call it even.

ANDY: I thought you hated liars.

LUPIE: Oh, I suppose you think you're clever now. Throwing my words in my face.

ANDY: Not at all.

LUPIE: If you're so clever, why travel hundreds of miles to babysit?

ANDY: I'm starting med school at Columbia in September. Didn't she tell you?

LUPIE: I see. It's a conspiracy.

ANDY: No, I just had nowhere to stay until classes started and your niece very kindly offered me this job. So can I please put my bags someplace?

LUPIE: I don't want you here!

ANDY: You think I want to be! You think this is the job of a lifetime?!

LUPIE: Don't you yell at me, you stupid little girl. I won't stand for it.

ANDY: You've been yelling at me since I got here.

LUPIE: That's my prerogative. I live here. You want to vent your spleen, you go across the street to that Chinese restaurant, tell them they're eating cats. I've seen them carting in kitties at 2 A.M. Go, save our pets. (ANDY slowly smiles.) Don't you smile at me.

(ANDY stops smiling as LUPIE defiantly puts the needle back on the record. 20s music plays. LUPIE's legs begin to spasm. She grabs at her knees to try to stop them as she struggles to stay in the wheelchair.)

LUPIE: Help!

(She reaches to take off the needle. Her hand slips and pushes it off the album with a violent scratch.)

ANDY: Lupie? LUPIE! *(Runs toward her)* What— what should I do?

LUPIE: Press down on my legs. Down. Harder.

(ANDY *presses down on* LUPIE'S *thighs. They slowly stop spasming.*)

Thank you. *(Beat)* What is your name again?

ANDY: Andy.

LUPIE: Short for Andrew?

ANDY: Andrea.

LUPIE: Oh. Andrew fits you better. You're very boyish.

ANDY: Gee wow, thanks.

LUPIE: I'm paying you a compliment.

ANDY: Hey Andy—you have no chest, waist, or hips?

LUPIE: Flappers were boyish. They behaved boyishly.

ANDY: Were you a flapper?

LUPIE: I most certainly was.

ANDY: So you cut off all your hair and jumped in fountains, things like that.

LUPIE: Yes. I would go straight from the barber to the nearest gushing statue.

ANDY: Do you always have to be facetious? Can't you take a break for like two minutes?

LUPIE: Do you know anything about flappers?

ANDY: What I got from school, reading Fitzgerald. This place looks like something right out of *Gatsby.*

LUPIE: Well, we were jumping into a lot better things than fountains.

ANDY: Like those great convertible cars with the spare tires on the back.

LUPIE: I was referring to sexual things.

ANDY: Oh.

LUPIE: No wonder my niece hired you. You're a prude, too.

ANDY: No, I'm not. It's just, I guess I don't think it's appropriate to refer to sexual things around someone so much older than me.

LUPIE: When did you lose your virginity?

ANDY: Jesus.

LUPIE: I rest my case.

ANDY: OK, literally or figuratively?

LUPIE: I have a choice?

ANDY: Literally, my horse refused a fence when I was thirteen and I landed point-blank on her withers, which rid me of my so-called maidenhead.

LUPIE: How painful. When was the penis?

ANDY: Nineteen.

LUPIE: Better late than never.

ANDY: It's not like I didn't have offers. I was waiting for the man of my dreams.

LUPIE: And he arrived?

ANDY: No, I just thought he'd be good in bed.

LUPIE: Was he?

ANDY: Not really. But I definitely feel fine about how old I was. And I don't think losing your virginity has anything to do with whether or not you're a prude.

LUPIE: Whatever.

ANDY: How old were you?

LUPIE: Fourteen.

ANDY *(Shocked):* Fourteen?

LUPIE: He was a soldier. Had just returned from France and was boasting about his experience with Parisian women. I told him to prove it.

ANDY: And he did?

LUPIE: Just barely. His penis was shaking so badly it was quite obvious he was lying.

ANDY: And you told him that?

LUPIE: Of course.

ANDY: Poor guy.

LUPIE: Oh, he did quite well for himself. Made a killing and married a Ziegfeld girl. *(Points to a picture frame)* He's in that photograph. Top row with a white beret.

(ANDY crosses to the frame.)

ANDY: Cute. Are you in here?

LUPIE: White lace and fuzzy.

ANDY *(Looking):* That could be anyone. What else are you wearing?

LUPIE: A moustache.

ANDY: A moustache?

LUPIE: Next to a man in a feather headband.

ANDY *(Pointing):* There! Oh, you were very beautiful, even with facial hair.

LUPIE: We were pretending to be incognito. My lover, Ernie, and I.

ANDY *(Looking closer):* So you slept with that guy.

LUPIE: Rarely. Our nick-names were Night and Owl.

ANDY *(Pointing):* Is that Edna St. Vincent Millay?

LUPIE: You're familiar with her?

ANDY: I majored in poetry.

LUPIE: Dear god, you aren't going to inflict your bad poems on me, are you?

ANDY: I don't write. *(Turning from picture)* Does that happen often? Your legs.

LUPIE *(Toughening up):* That's none of your business.

ANDY: Jesus, you still aren't going to admit you need my help?

LUPIE *(Rolling away):* I am going to bed.

ANDY: Fine, where should I sleep?

LUPIE: Look under the yellow pages for Women's Homeless Shelters. That's where people like you sleep in New York.

(ANDY grabs her wheelchair from behind.)

ANDY *(Shaking the chair for emphasis):* Listen, old lady. You want someone to shoot you up with sugar and keep you from falling out of your chair, you tell me where to fucking sleep.

LUPIE: Isn't there someone I can pay to take you in?

ANDY: Sorry, I've a wicked stepmother. And I promised your niece. She's my advisor. I'm not going to screw that up before classes even start.

(She pushes LUPIE away from her and goes for her bags.)

I'll find a bedroom.

(ANDY starts off. LUPIE turns, picks up a book, and throws it at her. ANDY freezes.)

LUPIE: Crap. I missed!

(ANDY slowly turns, drops her bags, and heads toward the telephone. She dials while feeling about in her jeans' pockets.)

ANDY: Shit! Where did I put it? *(Searches with growing frustration)* Shit shit. *(She drops the telephone and starts to dig into her bags.)* Where is it!!

LUPIE: Where is what?

ANDY *(Still digging):* Your niece's cellular number. Maybe I can stay in her apartment. You can keep having nurse's aides sent over every three hours 'til she gets back. See how you like a hundred of them messing with your stuff. *(Hand to forehead)* I know I had it. Shit!

> *(She throws down the bag and crosses out to the "balcony," which is delineated by moonlight. LUPIE picks up the telephone and rolls over to her cane. She puts it in her lap and rolls over to the shaken ANDY.)*

ANDY *(Seeing cane):* You gonna hit me with your cane now?

LUPIE: That's an antique telephone you dropped.

ANDY: My apologies.

LUPIE: Want a drink?

ANDY: No, thanks.

LUPIE: Then I'll have one.

> *(She unscrews the top of the cane and pours gin out of it into the top. She downs it.)*

ANDY: What is that?

LUPIE: Gin, what'd you think?

ANDY *(Beat):* Okay, pour me one.

> *(LUPIE pours ANDY a shot. She downs it.)*

ANDY: Ayyahaugh. That—is—so—hard.

LUPIE Isn't it though. *(LUPIE pours another shot and offers it to ANDY. She waves it away so LUPIE downs it.)*

ANDY: This—isn't—good for your sugar level.

LUPIE: Too bad. Now check in your shirt pocket.

ANDY: Huh?

LUPIE: For the number.

> *(ANDY checks and pulls out a little slip of paper.)*

ANDY: Fuck! Excuse me, but it just flips me out when that happens.

LUPIE: Get used to it. It only gets worse.

ANDY *(Brushing her off):* No, you don't get it.

LUPIE: You're telling a ninety-year-old woman she doesn't understand forgetfulness?

ANDY: It's not the same, I mean, that probably was, I was pissed off and blanked out, but forgetting means ending up in a room walking in circles and I don't want to get used to that if you don't mind. Excuse me. I'm exhausted. I promise not to injure any of your antique beds.

(She gets her bags and exits. LUPIE pours another shot and looks up at the moon.)

LUPIE: Wanna drink? *(Downs shot, replaces the cap)* Talk to me moon. Why am I still alive?

Time Zoned

MICHELLE A. GABOW

Two women, HARRIET and TANYA, find themselves in bed together. Their bed hangs from the ceiling, as if suspended in midair. Their ages are purposely left ambiguous, anywhere from thirty to sixty years old. HARRIET sees herself as a doer; TANYA is the dreamer. Yet, in bed, that too is subject to change. Bright lights. The morning after. HARRIET rolls over on her back. Her eyes move up toward the ceiling.

HARRIET: Damn. Where are we? When . . .What . . . Why did . . .

TANYA: You forgot how.

HARRIET: What?

TANYA: Not *what* was said. Just how.

HARRIET: Do you have any water?

(TANYA passes her a glass from the side of the bed. As HARRIET stretches out her hand for the glass, her covers drop and she pulls them up quickly over her nude breasts.)

OK. How?

TANYA: We were talking after work . . . How far should I go back . . .

HARRIET *(In recognition):* You're the new girl.

TANYA: Not any more . . .

HARRIET: In training . . .

(Both chuckle.)

HARRIET: God, I'm not even . . . I'm as heterosexual as they come.

TANYA: Could have fooled me.

HARRIET: What the hell were we drinking?

TANYA: It wasn't sloe gin fizz.

HARRIET: Is this part of your style? Because it's really getting boring fast.

TANYA: Sorry. I come up with one-liners when I'm nervous. A real Henny Youngman.

HARRIET: Who? I feel drugged. I can't seem to get out of bed. What time is it? *(TANYA shrugs.)* How old are we? *(TANYA shrugs.)* How did we get here?

TANYA: It happened too fast.

HARRIET: I am not fast.

TANYA: Neither am I. Nevertheless . . .

HARRIET: It seems just yesterday, getting high was new. When did it get old? Am I as old as you?

TANYA: Probably older.

HARRIET: How do you know?

TANYA: Everybody is.

HARRIET: You never change.

TANYA: Not really.

HARRIET: Well, look in the mirror.

TANYA: I don't need to look in mirrors. I've banned them all from my home.

HARRIET: I'd die without a mirror.

TANYA: Well . . .

HARRIET: Is that it? Are we dead? *(TANYA kisses her.)* Damn. We're living. Then . . . Who are we? *(TANYA shrugs.)*
    (Long pause.)

HARRIET: Is it time for a cigarette?

TANYA: Why not.
    (TANYA pulls herself by her hands to her footstool. This is a difficult task. She is struggling to reach her pack of cigarettes without losing touch with the bed. At one point, her whole body, with the exception of her feet, is off the bed.)

HARRIET: Is this our first time?

TANYA *(While struggling):* Feels like it to me.

HARRIET: I think it went very well then. How, 'bout you?

TANYA: You take my breath away. *(She lights two cigarettes and coughs.)*

HARRIET: Smoker's cough. *(TANYA shrugs.)* I'm sorry. I can't remember. Do I smoke or am I trying to stop?

TANYA: I think that you really want this Camel; it's terribly delicious after.

HARRIET: It makes your breath smell. I don't find that sexy. *(TANYA breathes into her hand and smells.)* We really shouldn't smoke. Isn't it against the law?

TANYA: Not in bed.

HARRIET: Well nevertheless.

TANYA: Jesus, we're against the law.

HARRIET: I don't think I smoke. I'm sure. Cancer is a horrible disease. It took out the female side of my family.

TANYA: Did they smoke?

HARRIET: I can't remember.

TANYA: Then what the hell. Indulge.

HARRIET: Oh God, I hate decisions. *(Pause)* I wonder if this was a conscious decision. Or did I just go with my intuition?

TANYA: What?

HARRIET: Us.

TANYA: Is life always this hard for you?

HARRIET: I think so.

TANYA: Do you, uh, foresee change?

HARRIET *(Defiantly):* Give me the damn cigarette!
(They silently smoke in bed.)

Nymphs of the Vernal Palette

MARY FENGAR GAIL

On an island off the coast of Maine stands an isolated house by the sea. Inside is an artist's studio where FAY LOCKE, age 15, is posing for her eccentric tutor, MURIEL DAUBLER, age 33. FAY's family is moving, but she wishes to remain on the island and live with MURIEL. MURIEL paints as FAY strikes a dramatic pose.

FAY: I'll stay with you. We could start a gallery of our own. We could work together!

MURIEL: Don't be silly. A new environment, a new school, they'll inspire you. Stand still!

FAY: You don't like me anymore.

MURIEL: Of course I do, but it's time you exposed yourself to other teachers.

FAY: But no one can teach me what you have! I've already made four commissions! Oh, Muriel, stop painting! How can we ever leave each other? Let's live together, here in your house.

MURIEL: Your parents wouldn't approve.

FAY: Who cares what they think?! Remember when you said how artists have to make every sacrifice to live under whatever conditions can make them grow?

MURIEL: Yes, and I have to live alone.

FAY: But why?

MURIEL: Because I do. It's my way. I need my space— for my paintings, my pacings, my moods. And Fay, darling, I'm afraid you've become too attached to me. *(She laughs.)* There, I'm finished: *My Flypaper Clown.*

FAY: What do you mean?

MURIEL: I'm finished for now. You can get dressed.

FAY: What do you mean, "my flypaper clown"?

MURIEL: Nothing. It's just my title for the painting.

FAY: Please, Muriel, don't make me leave.

MURIEL: Look, it's your parents' decision, not mine. And I'm afraid you've let our friendship become an infatuation. It's not at all uncommon in young girls. I care for you very much, but you're only fifteen for heaven's sake, and it's time to move on. These are crucial growing years.

FAY: But don't you want to watch me?

MURIEL: No, no I don't. I want to watch myself. Besides, I've seen how you've grown. You seem bent on continuing the academic traditions . . .

FAY: Which *you* taught me! You taught but *I* sell!

MURIEL: Who'd have thought I'd produce a commercial commodity?

FAY: You used to love my paintings! I was painting in the Grand Style when you said you adored me. You said it! You did! Adored! Adored! Adored!

MURIEL: Oh, so it's my fault that you're fixated there? That's ridiculous! Your problem is you love flattery. *(Mimicking Fay's mother)* "Oh, thank you, Miss Daubler. Everyone's so impressed with Fay's technique."

FAY: It's better than yours! My father says I could earn my own living.

MURIEL: Frankly, your earlier work was better. At least it wasn't so vain, so . . . so competent!

FAY: You think I'm nothing!

MURIEL: To be an artist, a real artist, it's not enough to fill garish walls with other people's expectations. You have to be selfish . . .

FAY: Like you!

MURIEL: You have to fulfill your own promise, which means going away and becoming a woman of the world! I admit you've been an educational experiment, and perhaps I've gone too far, but I feel . . . well, if you don't change, then I've failed.

FAY: Then give me another chance! *(Embracing her)* I still need you. Please!

MURIEL: I don't want to be needed. It's too much responsibility. I . . . I can't handle it; you're too . . . too passionate.

FAY: Yes! As passionate as Tintoretto! As Gauguin! *(Kissing her feverishly)* Love me, Muriel, love me. I'll never leave you, never! Never! Never!

MURIEL: Oh, darling, I . . . I can't. I just want to stay here and paint without accounting to anyone for anything. You're too young to want to begin all over again, but I'm not. You want me to give you a chance, well, give *me* a chance.

FAY: Is there someone else?

MURIEL: No, no, please stop it. *(Breaking away)* Leave me alone, please!

FAY *(Long pause; trembling):* If that's how you feel . . .

MURIEL: Yes.

FAY: Would you give me something? A present before I go?

MURIEL: Of course, anything.

FAY: "Anything!" Listen to you! You're so glad to get rid of me you can't even hide it!

MURIEL: Don't be silly. You can have whatever you want, Fay, you know that.

FAY: Anything?

MURIEL: I just told you, yes. What is it?

FAY: I want that painting you did, the mock Reubens you did of us, the one you called *Nymphs of the Vernal Palette.*

MURIEL: Oh. *(Pause)* It's very precious to me, but if you want it, it's yours. *(Whispering)* You can be its secret guardian.

FAY: Yes, we wouldn't want anyone to see it, would we? But don't worry, I know just where to hang it.

MURIEL: Where?

FAY: On the stake in my heart!!!

Mercy

LAURA HARRINGTON

ANNIE and LIZ are sisters. Their mother, Faith, is dying of cancer. LIZ is the perfect daughter with the perfect house, children, and husband (Macy). In this scene, she wears a scarf to cover the latest bruises inflicted by her perfect husband. ANNIE, who hasn't come to terms yet with her second sight, has been in flight from her family (including her brother, Daniel) and their tragic demons for the last five years. This is her first visit home. ANNIE and LIZ climb opposite sets of stairs to their mother's floor in the hospital. They meet outside Faith's room.

LIZ: Took you long enough.

ANNIE: Hello to you, too. *(They do not touch.)* God, I hate hospitals. Where's Dad?

LIZ: He's around. He checks in and out.

ANNIE: Are you all right?

LIZ: Yeah.

ANNIE: No you're not.

LIZ: I don't want to talk about it—

ANNIE: Macy?

LIZ: Don't shine your prying, know-it-all-eyes on me, girl.

ANNIE: I'm just *asking.*

LIZ: I said I don't want to talk about it.

ANNIE: Girls all right?

LIZ: They're fine.

> *(Beat)*

ANNIE: I can't go in there.

LIZ: Dad's walking his feet off.

ANNIE: Can you go in there?

LIZ: Every day.

ANNIE: Where are the kids?

LIZ: In the cafeteria. With the sitter.

ANNIE: Don't they—

LIZ: No.

ANNIE: They haven't seen her?!

LIZ: You don't know what she looks like. It's pretty bad—

ANNIE: To you, maybe—but your kids—they're just kids—what do they know?

LIZ: I don't want them to remember her like this—

ANNIE: Liz, maybe they're not going to remember her *at all*—

LIZ: It's none of your business, Annie. *(Pause)* You've put on weight again.

ANNIE: Score!

LIZ: I didn't mean it like that—

ANNIE: No, of course not. You, on the other hand, look great—

LIZ: Thanks.

ANNIE: Just pop those kids out and snap right back into shape, huh?

LIZ: It's not easy—

ANNIE: No . . . no . . . all those hours on the Stairmaster . . . Tell me . . . do you ever feel a sense of futility?

LIZ: Shut up, Annie.

ANNIE: Climbing and climbing, year after year, and never getting anywhere . . .

LIZ: You don't know anything about me.

ANNIE: You're right. I don't.

> *(Pause. ANNIE peeks in the door, takes a step forward, then back. Leans against the wall, breathless.)*

I'm here. I'm finally here . . . and now I can't go in there.

LIZ: It's you she wants. You and Daniel. I don't know why I keep going through the motions.

> *(She turns and walks away.)*

Skin

NAOMI IIZUKA

The boardwalk. The sun is a big white hole. The air is hot and still. The sounds of the radios and the cars cruising by all get lost in the folds of a dress. The ocean is a slit of bluest blue so narrow you forget it's even there. Men pass by with their shirts off and their eyes hidden behind dark glasses. MARY and LISA watch them.

MARY: I'm dreaming of men—

LISA: mary says to me, she says—

MARY: I'm dreaming of men beautiful men—

LISA: we're out in mission bay just hanging out, this was a long time ago, and it's hot and the sun is so bright everything looks warped and wavy like it's melting, and I can't even move, and mary tells me she tells me this crazy ass dream, she says she says to me—

MARY: I'm dreaming—

LISA: mary—

MARY: this was a long time ago—

LISA: mary—

MARY: I'm dreaming of men. they fall out of the sky. they fall and they crash into buildings and some of them get caught in the trees. some of them hit the ground and break into a lot of little pieces and I pick up all the pieces I see and I take them home with me and I sew the pieces all together anyway into this thing.

LISA: that's crazy.

MARY: and I think it's going to be this amazing thing, but it's ugly and fucked up and all I want to do is throw it away.

LISA: still.

MARY: and all I want to do, all I want to do.

LISA: the sound of water.

MARY: I'm dreaming of men.

LISA: the sound of water. this is a long time ago.

MARY: I listen to the men. they talk and laugh. I try to hear the words they say.

LISA: once upon a time, a long time ago.

MARY: it's so hot. I want to sleep.

LISA: last night I'm at work and this guy asks me if he can put his hand on my thigh for five bucks, and I tell him, you have got to be kidding, so then he says, ok I'll buy you a drink, and I'm like, ok whatever, so the hostess comes over and he pays, and then he says he'll give me ten bucks if he can put his hand on my thigh, and I say sure why not, and after a while I'm like, ok that's ten bucks worth, and he was cool, and then later, I saw he had a scar on his hand, and the skin was all smooth and see-through kind of, and I asked him how he got it, but he told me some bullshit story—

MARY: still.

LISA: and I thought, what an asshole you are, I'm asking you a fucking question, I'm looking for a fucking answer, asshole. what's it to you to tell me the truth.

MARY: I have a scar on my belly from when my baby was born. it didn't close up for a long time. now it's so white. when I touch it, it's all glossy, the skin, and shiny. sometimes I wake up and I think it hurts, but the doctor says it's all in my head. what time is it?

LISA: I don't know. late.

MARY: I'm hot.

LISA: I am so hot.

MARY: hey, look. look at that.

(they look off, seeing a Navy man. his head is shaved. his eyes are invisible behind dark green glass. there is a whole entire world in that dark glass, twisted and glowing.)

LISA: he's so fine.

MARY: mmhm.

LISA: I like that.

MARY: he is hot.

LISA: I like that. I do like that.

MARY: I swear I'd like a piece of that all for myself.

LISA: ssh.

MARY: what?

LISA: he heard you.

MARY: so?

LISA: he's looking at you, girl, he's looking you up and down. you see that?

MARY: I see.

(the Navy man goes away.)

LISA: you better watch yourself.

MARY: I'm just playing.

LISA: I saw how you were looking at him. I know what you're thinking.

MARY: oh?

LISA: just stick your eyes back into your head. do yourself a favor.

MARY: excuse me.

LISA: you know what I'm saying. don't act like you don't.

MARY: why don't you explain it all to me.

LISA: you know what it is.

MARY: I really don't.

LISA: please.

MARY: you want to fight?

LISA: I ain't the one fighting.

MARY: I think you're jealous. bitch.

LISA: please, you ain't all that.

MARY: I get what I want.

LISA: yeah you get knocked up is what you get.

MARY: fuck you. hag.

LISA: slut.

MARY: you better get out of my face before I kick your ass, bitch.

LISA: fuck you.

(LISA goes away.)

MARY: fuck you. fuck her.

The Parting of the Ways

CORINNE JACKER

ALICE and LEONA, both widows in their forties, are having a picnic in the country on the anniversary of the day ALICE's husband, Eddie, was killed by a random shooter. They are planning the wedding of ALICE's daughter, Julie. They have a Brides magazine.

LEONA: Nice here, isn't it?

ALICE: I guess.

LEONA: Beautiful day.

ALICE: Um-hmm.

LEONA: What's wrong?

ALICE: Nothing's wrong. Why does something have to be wrong?

LEONA: It usually is, isn't it.

ALICE: Usually. Not always.

LEONA: Your daughter all right?

ALICE: Fine. She adores law school, so she tells me.

LEONA: You have cancer or something?

ALICE: No. . . . Indigestion sometimes, that's all. I had my physical last week.

LEONA: Your forehead's as wrinkled as an unironed sheet.

ALICE: I'm thinking. . . about things. . . . It's a kind of anniversary.

LEONA: Oh. *(Pause)* I'm waiting.

ALICE: For what?

LEONA: For the other shoe to drop.

ALICE: I don't think I dropped the first one.

LEONA: Do me a favor. Please. Enjoy yourself today.

ALICE: I am.

LEONA: You could have fooled me.

ALICE: It's a year.

LEONA: Oh. You mean since Eddie died.

ALICE: Yes. I thought—you see, the picnic Eddie and I never got to eat. The meal I forgot. We forgot. The day we took the train. This was what I packed today. A kind of memorial.

LEONA: Damn it! You are morbid. What am I supposed to do? Drop dead?

ALICE: Not unless you feel like it.

LEONA: Why didn't you put Julie through this instead?

ALICE: She wouldn't understand.

LEONA: And I'm supposed to? Because I'm a widow? I don't eat Jeff's last meal every anniversary. He was in the hospital of course. Because of the medicine, all he could get down was lime Jell-O. I hate lime Jell-O.

ALICE: Well, I'm not all that fond of liverwurst.

LEONA: Punishing yourself?

ALICE: I suppose.

LEONA: After a year, you should be done with that.

ALICE: I will be. Don't rush me.

(Pause. LEONA looks around her.)

LEONA: Well, this beats 74th Street. Thanks for bringing me out here.

ALICE: You're welcome.

LEONA: Everybody in New York needs the country sometime. Especially this time of year. All the buds on the trees.

ALICE: And forsythia. The forsythia's in full flower. The lilac's budding.

LEONA: Christ! We sound like a PBS nature series for kids.

ALICE: I like nature series. Julie and Eddie watched them all the time. . . .

LEONA: I've been watching the geese.

ALICE: All right. We'll change the subject. Do you think they're pretty or just foolish?

LEONA: Pretty. Dumb but pretty. Oh, look, they've got little—what-do-you-call-ums?

72

ALICE: Goslings. See how they take them out. The mother in front, and then the goslings, and then the father.

LEONA: How do you know the father doesn't go first?

ALICE: Did you know that geese mate for life? Look. See that one on the far side, by itself. All alone. It travels with the family. Maybe it's a widow.

LEONA: Or a spinster. Whatever.

ALICE: But it's going to be alone for the rest of its life. Just traveling along, pretending its got kids.

LEONA: For God's sake, Alice. We're in the country for a day. Relax, won't you?

ALICE: The country makes me melancholy, I guess.

LEONA: Please.

ALICE: OK. . . . Want to play some horseshoes? Or maybe some Scrabble?

LEONA: Occupational therapy.

ALICE: I'm sorry I'm putting you through all this. . . . Want another piece of cake—a cookie?

LEONA: I *want* it, but I won't have it.

ALICE: Admirable. *(ALICE takes a cookie herself.)*

LEONA: Alice—I've—uh, listen. I want to tell you something. *(ALICE looks curiously at her.)* A secret. Well, sort of a secret. More a confidence, you'd call it.

ALICE: You met somebody.

LEONA: How did you know?

ALICE: You can't be pregnant. . . . Is he nice?

LEONA: He's OK.

ALICE: Just OK?

LEONA: Well, that's better than being a total nerd isn't it? His name's Alan. Alan Stern. He's about six feet tall and he's bald and—oh, don't laugh, please don't laugh—he's an undertaker.

ALICE: How did you ever meet an undertaker?

LEONA: On the crosstown bus. The driver was one of those real jocks, you know. Starting and stopping. And Al just fell in my lap.

ALICE: Fate!—That's how Eddie died you know. In my lap.

LEONA: Don't make fun. Maybe it's karma or something. He's a Leo. There couldn't be a better sign for me. Anyway. We talked, and he insisted on buying me a coffee, and one thing led to another, and we went to see *Pulp Fiction*, which he hated by the way and we argued for about half an hour. And he called me, and we went to the movies again, and—

ALICE: You slept together. And now you're having all kinds of fantasies.

LEONA: Umm-hmm. Like an ironic romance or something. Being an undertaker's girlfriend.

ALICE: Does he at least have a sense of humor?

LEONA: I don't know. There hasn't been anything to laugh at yet. He's been— his wife died five years ago.

ALICE: And?

LEONA: It's so niggling. I don't know how to tell him. He has— he sort of has bad breath.

ALICE: Dentures?

LEONA: I suppose, maybe. But at least he's a person between the sheets. . . . Not bad in the sex department, either. I mean, it's a good compromise. *(ALICE begins to feed the geese.)* You still feed the birds. . . . You don't approve. Of me and Alan.

ALICE: I'm like the geese. Monogamous for life.

LEONA: I bet some birds don't have any ethics, just sleep around like crazy.

ALICE: It's not ethics.

(LEONA picks up Brides *magazine.)*

LEONA: There. Look at that one. Everything. The color, the line.

ALICE: Look at the price. I'm not— ·

LEONA: It's you.

ALICE: No it isn't.

LEONA: How many gorgeous dresses do you think there are in mauve? Julie did say mauve, didn't she?

ALICE: Now you're acting like the mother of the bride. . . . Did she want mauve? Oh, I guess she did. But—a thousand dollars? For one night.

LEONA: It's the most important day of her life.

ALICE: So . . . She's the one who has to look gorgeous, not me.

LEONA: Don't start nickel-and-diming me. Take my advice. Look good while you can. Another couple of years and you'll be at Roseland, dying to dance one dance with somebody.

ALICE: I'd look like, you know, Shirley MacLaine when she goes on talk shows.

LEONA: She must be almost seventy years old. Besides. You're supposed to look special.

ALICE: I didn't mean special. Old in sheep's clothing.

LEONA: Look who's wearing the dress. It's Mrs. Exeter, sort of. You're mother of the bride. And you'll have the money any day now. You've got the settlement coming from the railroad.

ALICE: I don't know if I want anything. What kind of bastards figured how much Eddie was worth by the ounce? Don't count your awards till you see the whites of their money.

LEONA: Hunh?

ALICE: It was a joke. I was mixing my metaphors.

LEONA: It's an open-and-shut case. They should have had gun detectors or something so they wouldn't have let him on the train.

ALICE: I don't know. Suppose the guy ahead of him had been stopped because he had a fancy ballpoint pen.

LEONA: Loss of income, personal suffering, mental damage, your shrink's bills—of course you need the money.

ALICE: You sound like a lawyer.

LEONA: What would Eddie want you to do?

ALICE: Take the money, I suppose. But he's not here. I don't know what to do. We weren't big on hypothetical lawsuits as our pillow talk.

LEONA: Well—

ALICE: And we aren't now. . . . Leona, when your husband died—did you talk to him and everything?

LEONA: For a while. Then he . . . I don't know how to describe it. He got blurrier and blurrier.

ALICE: That's terrible.

LEONA: They say it takes about two years. It took me about that long. Then one morning, you wake up and you realize you

75

haven't thought about him for two days, or, wait, maybe it's more. "When was the last time I thought about him?" you think, and you can't remember.

ALICE: He'll probably go away when I go back to school. Then there won't be much for us to talk about. If I go back to school.

LEONA: You just said you were going.

ALICE: I don't know. I don't know what's right.

LEONA: You're just feeling the emptiness. That's where Al comes in handy. I'm bored. I'm tired of eating dinner alone. I want a buddy. A buddy I can sleep with.

ALICE: I'd be your buddy. Not to sleep with or anything like that. A kind of one, I mean. You could move in with me and take care of me while I go to class and study and write my dissertation.

LEONA: I need another kind of buddy, Alice. I don't want to be a housewife. He'll take me on trips to Jamaica or Europe. He'll take me to movies and out to dinner. And I'll feel like somebody wants me again. You'll see. Wait a while.

ALICE: I don't feel sexually frustrated. Is that a part of it all— being a widow? Do your juices start flowing again? I mean, Eddie and me—we loved one another, don't get me wrong, but we screwed maybe every two weeks, at best. Tell me is there a whole etiquette I have to learn? Some kind of polite widow behavior then? I don't even know the language yet.

LEONA: You'll find out. It comes naturally. But you have to compromise. Like going out on a date. Don't strain your brain reading that biology stuff. It doesn't make for light conversation. Soon you'll be out playing mixed-couple bridge with the rest of us.

ALICE: I don't want to make light conversation.

LEONA: I was there ahead of you. I know how you'll be. I can tell you what's best for you.

ALICE: You sound like Eddie. Making me up as you go along.

LEONA: I'm telling you, you're just feeling—by yourself. After Julie's married, take a trip to Alaska, or Machu Picchu, or

China. . . . OK. So that's my kind of solution. Maybe you don't want somebody dumb and normal like me for a buddy.

ALICE: You're not dumb! I love having a normal pal like you.

(She hugs LEONA, who smiles, shows her another page in the magazine.)

LEONA: I feel, kind of odd showing you this, but look—you wear that necklace with the dress and—it's a knockout.

ALICE: Leona, maybe we should do this some other time. . . . I don't think I want to look like a knockout right now.

LEONA: But you have to. It's Julie's wedding.

ALICE: And Eddie's not giving her away. Her uncle is.

LEONA: Yeah. Sorry.

ALICE: You should be! *(Slight pause)* Lee. I'm sorry. I know you love her and all. But—

LEONA: Yeah, I know. She's all you have left. You sure as hell have a funny way of showing it. Why don't you tell her that?

ALICE: I can't. I mean if I did, I think I might just crumble up and blow away or something. Look what showing Eddie what I felt got us.

LEONA: Stop that! I thought you got all that straightened out with the shrink. Killing him, I mean. You were an innocent bystander.

ALICE: I'm alive. He's long dead. What's so innocent about that?

LEONA: Look. Right now, I could walk to the edge of this cliff and lose my balance and fall off. Would you have killed me?

ALICE: Depends. If I could have reached you and I was afraid and didn't even reach out my hand.

LEONA: First you're wound up so tight you'll break and then you sound like Julie being lawyerly.

ALICE: OK. I wasn't responsible. Have it your way. But I'm not going to dance on Eddie's grave.

LEONA: Enough with the mourning.

ALICE: Leona, please. Help.

LEONA: Not now. Now we have to think about Julie. It's about time she enjoyed herself, too. She's almost graduated. She's getting married next month. Make it a good wedding, Alice.

ALICE: Damn her! Why couldn't she have made her mind up last year. We would never have gone on the trip. And Eddie would be here to talk reasonably to her about whether the whole thing is such a good idea. He should give her away himself. It should be his job. All of it. . . . Why can't she just elope or something?

LEONA: What are you so mad about?

ALICE: Eddie isn't here. I can't remember the last time I talked to him. Yesterday, or maybe over the weekend. Maybe he is getting blurry, like you said.

LEONA: That's a part of it, the mourning, after a while you get over being crazy.

ALICE: I don't want to get over it! I like being crazy. It's nice and safe.

LEONA: What's wrong with you?

ALICE: Me? Nothing. I'm overjoyed.

LEONA: It is the wedding. It's Tim, isn't it?

ALICE: He's all right. He's respectable enough to show to the guests. Fine for sitting next to me at the wedding dinner. But how do I know if he's the one to make Julie happy for the rest of her life?

LEONA: So? That's for her to find out.

ALICE: I'm afraid. She'll have the degree, and a job, but she'll quit thinking she wants to be a lawyer and spend years making a nice home for him, and she'll have a kid or two and read about big courtroom cases in the paper and daydream about the ones she could be handling while she changes the diapers. And years later he'll get on a train and there'll be some guy who starts shooting at random. Or he'll come home from work from one day with a headache and the headache won't go away and when he goes to the doctor it'll turn out to be a brain tumor. Or—whatever—something will kill him. I'd feel better if she was going to be a nun.

LEONA: We don't have any guarantees, do we? Who knows if you'll be at the wedding. Maybe I'll tell you a joke and you'll laugh so hard you have a heart attack. What's so special about being alive?

ALICE: Yeah. I thought about that. Of killing myself, I mean.

LEONA: Don't be so ridiculous. OK. Forget about getting a buddy. Go back to school if you want.

ALICE: Well, when I picked, I picked Eddie, and I forgot all about the miracles of the cell. And after we got married I was monogamous. I never cheated on him. I never went to a lecture. I never opened a biology book.

LEONA: That is such a load of romantic crap. . . . Like you think there's some sort of divine plan. One mate. One career. One thing in a life. What there is is one life!

ALICE: This business about going back to school; I started reading the stuff again because I didn't have anything else to do and found out I like it. So, see, I really am enjoying myself, my way.

LEONA *(Shrugs):* I think you're kidding yourself. But—honey, I'm just trying to help. Honest.

ALICE: OK. Help me then. The best way you can help is to let me be.

LEONA: Why are you so busy turning people down?

ALICE: Me? I don't do that.

LEONA: Yes, you do. I'm trying and you want to walk away. Julie—she's getting married, without her father, and you could help her take some joy—who cares how it's going to turn out? Now's now, and she wants to be loved. Not just by Tim, by you, too, but you're so afraid of loving that you just turn away, so she comes to me. Well, as long as I'm alive the door to my place is open.

ALICE: I don't. It's just . . . Maybe I'm not in a wedding mood is all.

LEONA: Oh, no, you're in a mood to feel guilty because his dying was your fault. Well, maybe it was, but he's dead and who the hell cares whether you had anything to do with it. I'm tired of the subject.

ALICE: Wait a minute—

LEONA: No. Just stop whining, will you?

ALICE: I'm not whining. I'm crying.

Things That Break

SHERRY KRAMER

The waiting room at St. Mary's Hospital. ELIZABETH DEMERY is sitting on the sofa. She is in her early fifties. On the floor beside her is an ample knitting bag, filled to overflowing with yarn and half-knitted projects. Her husband is in the operating room, having open-heart surgery. JACKIE sits in a chair nearby. She is in her late twenties. Her father is in the operating room, having open-heart surgery.

ELIZABETH *(Looking up from her knitting, talks directly to the air in front of her):* This is killing me. *(Resumes knitting, calmly)* This is killing me.

> *(NURSE PITKIN enters, wearing a crisp cotton nurse's uniform more from the forties than the present, including one of those fabulous white caps. She flings open the door leading into the theatre, from the back of the house, and sweeps down the aisle. Everything about her manner suggests that she is in absolute charge, and we will all be just fine.)*

NURSE PITKIN: Hello. I'm Nurse Pitkin. And the first thing I'd like to say, is that all our patients are special. *(Beat)* But all their stories are the same.

JACKIE: I was on my way up to my father's room in the hospital, before the operation. I was on the elevator. The doors opened. A woman stepped in. She was—I don't know. Sixty-five. Seventy. But seventy the way seventy is in the farmland of our fairy tale American myth. Her faded hair was braided, and wrapped tightly at the back of her neck. Her face was— careworn. Right out of the movies. Auntie Em in *The Wizard of Oz* looked less like Auntie Em than she did.

ELIZABETH: This is killing me. Except, of course, that it might not be killing me. Everything might turn out all right, in which case, this would not be killing me. In which case, this would just be—making me strong. After all, what doesn't kill you, makes you strong.

(*She has ascended onto the stage.*)

NURSE PITKIN: I can say this, because I'm the Head Story Nurse here at St. Mary's. St. Mary's. The hospital with the three Cs—Care, Concern, and Compassion—engraved in granite on the admitting room wall.

JACKIE: She was wearing a cotton print dress, calico or plaid, washed a thousand times. She was straight, and tall, and there was a plain gold band on her left hand.

ELIZABETH: I think that *that's* what's killing me. Yes. That's it. What is killing me is not knowing whether this is killing me, or making me strong.

NURSE PITKIN: I wasn't always a Story Nurse. For a long time, I was June Pitkin, Head Dialysis Nurse. It was a rewarding, fulfilling charge.

JACKIE: And she was fine, until she stepped onto the elevator. But as soon as the doors slid shut she started to break. And I was standing right there, I didn't know what to do.

NURSE PITKIN: I had the hands for the work. I had the patience—with a C—for the patients—with a T—but I soon found out that kidney problems were too local, too limiting for me. And when a kidney breaks down—well, just look at the way the word breaks down. Kidneys—K-I-D-N-E-Y-S.
kid kids keys
den dens
din dines
sin kin
kind kinds
send ends
ski skid sky
ides side
dies . . .

You'd be amazed at how many words have dying in them. You really would. Almost as if the language had a death wish, built right in.

Let's see now, where was I . . . *(She goes through her fingers, remembering where she was)* side, die, dies . . . that's only twenty-five. And there are forty-nine anagramic possibilities using the letters in the word "kidneys." I'm twenty-four short.

ELIZABETH: After all, if it turns out that this is killing me, rather than just making me strong, that's exactly what I'll have to be. Because if everything I have ever believed is true, I won't have any choice. I'll have to be strong.

JACKIE: She had used up everything to make it into that elevator, she'd walked those steps to the door at unimaginable cost, she had lasted until the doors closed and what could I say to her? What words would I use? What was the use of any of the words I knew.

(NURSE PITKIN has been going through the list under her breath, trying out other combinations to find the missing words.)

NURSE PITKIN: . . . dei . . . dey . . . nei . . . oh, hell. It just goes to show you how far I've put kidney work behind me. And who wouldn't, really, if given the chance? What's dialysis all about, really. . . . I'll tell you. You clean out the machine, you hook up the patient, you clean out the patient, you unhook the patient, you clean out the machine. It's assembly line work.

JACKIE: I started to reach out, but I couldn't touch her. I asked her, "Is there anything I can do, Ma'am?" She shook her head.

NURSE PITKIN: It's still just nuts and bolts. It's still just connect this to that. This to that. Thisness and thatness.

JACKIE: She sobbed, and the elevator climbed forever, three floors, forever. At last the doors slid open, and somehow I stepped out. I walked blindly—just like they do in novels—blindly down the hall. I made it to my father's room, and I told him about the woman in the elevator. About how she had stood there, and just shattered.

And for the first time in my life, about a woman he had never even met and whose story he would never know, I saw my father cry.

ELIZABETH: I think, now that I really think about it, that *that's* what is killing me. Yes. What is really killing me is— *(It just barely, precisely, eludes her.)* Damn. I need to get this right, I really do. What doesn't kill you makes you strong . . . bullshit! *(She covers her mouth with her hand, shocked at herself for even thinking such a word.)* Bullshit. Bullshit. *(She's enjoying it.)* Bull . . . shit. I never really thought the word "bullshit" before. "Damn" and "hell" were as far as I had to go.

NURSE PITKIN: But, to make a long story short—I got out of this and that. I traded all of that and this in, for the overall narrative. The scope, the scale, and the larger casts, that come with the duties of the Head Story Nurse.

(Gradually, the three women become the woman in the elevator, adding small parts of her costume as they go.)

The day I met him—all the pieces of the world fell into place. I could almost feel the click.

ELIZABETH: Now I could stop struggling to make sense out of things—oh, just because you grow up on a farm doesn't mean you don't think, you know. Just because you rise with the sun—-and the barnyard animals are your friends—

JACKIE: —doesn't mean you don't think. So I did think. About a lot of things. And the minute I met him, I knew I could stop thinking about most of 'em.

ELIZABETH: You might think a person would be ashamed to say that, right out. But I'm not. I was happy and proud to have a man standing beside me who meant that I could stop thinking and worrying and get down to things.

NURSE PITKIN: To the real things.

ELIZABETH: Someone to work beside me.

JACKIE: Someone to pull together with and never worry about my back, and never worry there was no one on my side.

NURSE PITKIN: A partner for the day and its work, and the night and its rest.

ELIZABETH: He was a good man. A good husband, good father. I could almost hear that little click nine, ten times a day.

JACKIE: I didn't have to think about things, or put them together—

NURSE PITKIN: They were already put.

JACKIE: They made sense.

ELIZABETH: I'm not saying that I ever fully understood about the night, though.

JACKIE: I didn't have to give the day and its work a second thought—

ELIZABETH: —but the night and its rest—

NURSE PITKIN: That click was different. I never really understood that portion of our lives, what happened at night, between us, I never understood.

JACKIE: I'd thought about it quite a lot before we'd gotten married, no different than any other seventeen-year-old girl—

ELIZABETH: —and I was relieved to be able to stop thinking about it, once I realized it was nothing you could really think about. But the night and its rest—

NURSE PITKIN: I never understood it the way I understood the day—except I knew that it was good.

ELIZABETH: People talk about it all the time, sex, sex, sex, but they never say, "It's good—good the way work is, and bringing up three strong healthy children is, and having the respect of your neighbors, and standing for something is."

NURSE PITKIN: No one ever says that about it.

ELIZABETH: But it's true.

NURSE PITKIN: There's something I don't quite understand about it, but I know that's true.

ELIZABETH: I can still fit into my wedding dress. I know you hear a woman say that, you feel kind of sorry for them, you think, just another sad, old dried-up woman with all the sweetness sweated out of her, bragging about fitting into an old yellowed dress no one alive even remembers her wearing.

JACKIE: But it's not bragging.

NURSE PITKIN: Not vanity either, or pride.

ELIZABETH: It's just this little voice inside you saying, "I'm still the same person I was that day."

NURSE PITKIN: "I'm still standing in front of the preacher with my whole life ahead of me. I'm young and strong and I'm ready to pay."

JACKIE: "I am ready for the work, and I will pay."

ELIZABETH: So. I can still fit into my wedding dress.

NURSE PITKIN: I can still feel what I felt that day.

ELIZABETH: Let me go back and stand there again, I'll say it again. I'll still say I'll pay.

JACKIE: I'll work hard, with this man beside me, and between us, we'll pay.

ELIZABETH: And I knew, in the back of my mind, that this day—today—would come—that this day was part of it—

NURSE PITKIN: What I had to pay—

JACKIE: Part of the price you have to pay for standing there beside him.

ELIZABETH: I'm not saying I didn't know that the day would come when he wouldn't be there, beside me—I understood that the day would come, and I would stand here, alone—but I didn't realize, somehow, that he wouldn't be there during the night.

NURSE PITKIN: As if I understood part of what death is, but had completely left the other part out.

ELIZABETH: The day and its work, the night and its rest.

JACKIE: There they are, right together, you don't get one without the other.

ELIZABETH: They talk about it all the time, but they never really tell you. They tell you all kinds of stories, but the stories never tell you so you know.

NURSE PITKIN: They tell you all kinds of stories—

JACKIE: But the stories never tell you so you know.

ELIZABETH: I just didn't know about the night. That's all I'm saying.

NURSE PITKIN: And not a single story tells you so you know.

JACKIE: That's all I'm saying.

ELIZABETH: That's all I'm saying.

NURSE PITKIN: That's all I'm saying.

(*Blackout*)

Little Rhonda

ARDEN TERESA LEWIS

A mother and daughter at their summer beach house on the first morning after their arrival. MARION is practicing Spanish with a tape in the hopes of "connecting" with her teenage daughter, AMY. AMY would prefer to be left alone to read her books, but MARION is determined to draw her out of her shell. MARION is doing the sunbathing thing on the sand between the deck and the dune stage left. This includes hat, glasses, Vogue *magazine, headphones, and the tape player.*

MARION: Donde esta Suzanna? *(Beat)* Suzanna esta en la casa. La casa? . . . su casa.

    (A sleepy AMY comes out carrying a book. She sees her mother.)

AMY: Jesus Christ.

MARION: That you Amy?

AMY: Good guess.

    (Amy plops into a chair and opens her book.)

MARION: Oh, shoot . . . Suzanna esta en la biblioteca! Amy?

AMY: No, it's Madonna.

MARION: Oh, shit, now I'm behind. How do you stop this—

    (MARION struggles to stop the tape. She finally drops it. Spanish blares out from the machine.)

TAPE: Suzanna esta en la cocina!

MARION: Shit! *(MARION rips out the tape.)* There. I've killed it. *(AMY laughs.)* Amy? *(AMY stops laughing.)* Buenas Dias. *(Beat)* Yes, and a good morning to you too, mother. *(Beat)* Louise and I are going shopping later. We've heard about this new T-shirt artist who is wonderfully talented. She does these beautiful beach scenes in acrylics. Front and back, and I thought that sounded much more interesting than tie-dyeing.

AMY: No one tie-dyes anymore.

MARION: Exactly, so Louise and I thought this would be something different. *(Beat)* She also does watercolors. *(Beat)* Full paintings of course. Watercolor on a T-shirt would just, wash out. In water. *(Beat)* You used to do some beautiful watercolors. Amy?

AMY: Mom?

MARION: How about it?

AMY: How about what?

MARION: Would you like to go with us?

AMY: No.

MARION: But Amy—

AMY: Mom, you want to go, so you go.

MARION: You can't just sit around all day. We could work on our Spanish. You have to take that next year.

AMY: I'm going to take Samoan.

MARION: Oh. Samoan?

AMY: It's more romantic.

MARION: I don't think they have Berlitz tapes in Samoan.

AMY: Samoan girls are not civilized and boring.

MARION: Like American girls.

AMY: They can live anywhere they want. If they don't like their parents, they can move.

MARION: They also do all the cleaning, cooking and baby-sitting.

AMY: They do not!

MARION: Finish that book. Then see if you want to move out.

AMY: You've read Margaret Mead?

MARION: I do work in education, Miss Island Expert.

AMY: You're a secretary.

MARION: Yes, well even secretaries read occasionally.

AMY: All you ever read are women's magazines.

MARION: Well lately I've slacked off.

AMY: Lately?

MARION: Alright like the last ten years— But I'm very glad you are not taking my bad example and are reading something worthwhile.

AMY: She was brilliant.

MARION: Yes.

AMY: She felt a woman really needed four different men in her life.

MARION: Only four?

AMY: One to just have sex with.

MARION: Oh great.

AMY: One to bear children with, one to raise them, *and* one to grow old and die with.

MARION: I'm sure the men in her life loved this theory.

AMY: Where are your men, Mom?

MARION: What?

AMY: You don't have any men.

MARION: I had your father.

AMY: That's one.

MARION: WELL, I had sex before I met your father.

AMY: OK, two.

MARION: Your father was both the man to bear children with and raise them.

AMY: Wrong. He's not raising me.

MARION: Amy! Your father was a wonderful Daddy.

AMY: I don't even remember him. And it's abnormal that you haven't even been on a date in like forever.

MARION: How do you know what's normal? Because that's the way naked tribal people live that's normal? So I should bare my breasts and find a man to die with?

AMY: Yes! Bare your breasts, Mother, and dance in the fire again!
(Marion grabs the book.)

MARION: I'm returning these books and finding you some normal friends! There's got to be someone your own age on this island. I'm going to call Louise and tell her to bring over her neighborhood council list and go through it. And after that you are coming with us to our own little American village!

AMY: Mom!

MARION: What?

AMY: I hate Louise.

MARION: Don't be ridiculous. She's my best friend. She was your favorite baby-sitter.

AMY: I was too young to know any better.

MARION: Oh please.

AMY: When you two get together you're always bugging me about which boys I'm dating, or telling me what colors I should be wearing.

MARION: Don't like a taste of your own medicine. *(MARION gathers her things.)*

AMY: You'll paint me into a purple box of spring if I let you have your way.

MARION: Oh, you're so dramatic.

AMY: In a cage of vertical stripes!

MARION: Ame.

AMY: No prints allowed!

MARION: Stop it!

   (MARION reaches for AMY and starts dropping everything.)

AMY: Geometric heaven!

MARION: Amy! Shut up! *(AMY grabs her knapsack.)*

AMY: "Amy shut up"? Shut up? How can I realize my potential if you bury me in the mundane?!

   (AMY exits.)

MARION: Amy? . . . Amy!

Reincarnation

JESSICA LITWAK

ROSIE, a suicidal receptionist who has been diligently searching for true love, has recently been fired from her job. She has been lured, against her better judgment, into the storefront shop of a "Psychic Fortune Teller" in midtown Manhattan. She suddenly finds herself face to face with a greasy gypsy woman named MADAME CEUILI who wears a leopard skin housecoat and a turban, and speaks with a thick Romanian accent.

MADAME CEUILI: Fifty.

ROSIE: Dollars?

MADAME CEUILI: Everybody charges. Ask.

ROSIE: Fifty dollars is an enormous amount of money.

MADAME CEUILI: Do or don't do. That's the price.

ROSIE: I can't pay that much. I have rent and dating expenses. Subway tokens and egg salad sandwiches . . . and . . .

MADAME CEUILI *(Interrupting):* Visa. Mastercard. No personal check.

ROSIE: . . . I just lost my job.

MADAME CEUILI: I read hands, face, body hair. Fortune. Healing. Fix up de mess. God will work miracle, Lady, but you got to meet him halfway. *(Pause)* Forty-five dollar.

ROSIE: Forty-five?

MADAME CEUILI: I see everything.

ROSIE: What color underpants am I wearing?

MADAME CEUILI: White. Embroidery says Saturday even though it's Tuesday afternoon.

ROSIE: Jesus.

MADAME CEUILI: Madame Ceuili can help you, Judith.

ROSIE: How did you know . . . ?

MADAME CEUILI *(Interrupting):* I know everything.

ROSIE: Well no you don't because that's NOT my name.

MADAME CEUILI: SO?

ROSIE: So I do not call myself Judith. I call myself . . . *(Seeing if MADAME can guess)* . . . ROSIE!!!

MADAME CEUILI: Whatever you want. I'm a busy woman.
> *(MADAME CEUILI takes a sip of her coffee, turning slightly away from ROSIE, playing it cool.)*

ROSIE: Well, can you tell me anything about my love life?

MADAME CEUILI: No problem, Lady.

ROSIE: And the possibility of future happiness?

MADAME CEUILI: Sure, sure. Love life. Happiness.

ROSIE: Well . . .

MADAME CEUILI *(With a sigh):* Forty dollar. Last chance.

ROSIE: OK. All right. I hope I don't regret this . . .
> *(ROSIE digs through her pockets and comes up with some cash. She counts out forty dollars and holds it out to MADAME CEUILI.)*

MADAME CEUILI: Hold the money in your hand and make two wishes.
> *(ROSIE closes her eyes. Then nods and opens them. MADAME CEUILI grabs the cash and stuffs it in her bra. She motions ROSIE to a chair.)*

MADAME CEUILI: What did you wish for?

ROSIE: Don't you know?

MADAME CEUILI: Gonna get smart ass?
> *(Pause)*

ROSIE: Inner peace. And a boyfriend.

MADAME CEUILI: Big wish. Need much assistance. Lemme see your hands. *(She grabs ROSIE's hands and places them palm up on her lap.)* Oh God. Oh boy.

ROSIE: What's wrong?

MADAME CEUILI: Very bad. Head and heart line all mushed close together. CAUTION! WATCH OUT! Little lines here. Anxiety ALL around you. Confide in NO ONE. People talk behind your back. Natter natter. One lady wishes you very bad. Boss lady. Did you lose your job?

ROSIE: I just told you I did.

MADAME CEUILI: Life line broken here. Bad luck. Accident in subway. Lots of smoke.

ROSIE: What?

MADAME CEUILI: Let me see your eyes. Yep. Pig eyes. Like I thought. Bloodshot running all the way to center. Death in near future. Big accident.

ROSIE: Oh God. When?

MADAME CEUILI: Soon. Need to light a special emergency candle. Can you give up something so I can say important emergency prayer to discourage inevitable misfortune?

ROSIE: Give up what?

MADAME CEUILI: Each candle five dollar.

ROSIE: I just gave you forty.

MADAME CEUILI: Very bad accident. Bleeding from head. No one comes. Long death. Lying in pool of blood on subway floor, much old urine and chewing gum.

ROSIE: OK. OK.

(She gives MADAME CEUILI five dollars. MADAME CEUILI shoves it down her bra. She lights a candle with a little BIC lighter she takes out of a pocket. She replaces the lighter and takes up ROSIE's hands again.)

MADAME CEUILI: Soft here under mount of Venus. Pudgy. Like to please everybody. But look fingers bend in toward middle, means nobody likes you back. Head line slopes down here. That's good. You speak wise words. But star on mount of Jupiter mean no one listens to anything you say. . . . Let me see your eyebrows. Mmmm. Thick. Dark. Hair grows all which way. Very bad luck with opposite sex. Mortal silk worm eyebrow, little dragon on the tail. You want to be popular but men don't like the way you smell. Lamb eyes. Live long life, but live it all alone.

ROSIE: I thought you said I had pig eyes and was going to die on the subway.

MADAME CEUILI: We fix that one with special candle. Now must take curse off heart line. Five more dollar for special prayer.

ROSIE: Five more?

MADAME CEUILI: You want boyfriend or not? *(ROSIE coughs up five more bucks. MADAME CEUILI lights another candle.)* Let's see . . . lower lip bigger than top lip, means you want a husband with big arms. You got long rough hair. Not satisfied with just one man so make wrong choice three times. Water shape body. Willow leaf in stream. Will marry late but family disown you. Some hair on chin. Marriage not successful unless husband likes homosexual . . .

ROSIE: What?

MADAME CEUILI *(Continuing):* Cow shape nose. You will have children but they will grow up to hate you and become incarcerated for drug-related crimes . . .

ROSIE: Can you can fix all this for another five bucks?

MADAME CEUILI: Catching wind ears. Means unlucky with money. Poverty stricken. Die of hunger at age 50. Must light many candies to take away so many curses. Very bad. Many candles.

ROSIE: How many candles?

MADAME CEUILI: At least five.

ROSIE: That's twenty-five dollars!

MADAME CEUILI: I'll make you deal, Lady. Such a mess. Eighteen dollars for all. Special price.

ROSIE: I've already spent fifty dollars!

MADAME CEUILI: You need it bad. Big mess. Unhappy life. Die hungry. Pains in stomach . . . unemployed . . .

ROSIE *(Interrupting):* OK, OK, that's enough. I can't do this anymore. . . . This is ridiculous. I'm going to kill myself.

(ROSIE starts rummaging around in her purse. She pulls out a long rope in the shape of a noose, a bottle of poison, razor blades, a plastic bag, a knife, an axe, and some D-Con mouse killer. All the time ROSIE is removing objects, she is muttering to herself hopelessly. MADAME CEUILI is aghast. She speaks over ROSIE.)

MADAME CEUILI: Hey, hey wait. Lady. Hold on. Don't do nothing like that in my shop. Very bad luck. Big mess. Put back. Stop. Hey! Look. I got something. I got something else.

Something Big! HEY WAIT A MINUTE! I GOT THE
ANSWER TO YOUR PROBLEMS!

(ROSIE looks up.)

ROSIE: What?

MADAME CEUILI: Reincarnation.

ROSIE: Reincarnation?

MADAME CEUILI: It's the only way.

ROSIE: The only way?

MADAME CEUILI: To save you.

ROSIE: You can save me?

MADAME CEUILI: Maybe if go back, see what's gumming up the
works.

ROSIE: Huh?

MADAME CEUILI: Something very messed up with your past
lives.

ROSIE: Something is very messed up with my present life.

MADAME CEUILI: We gotta go back there, take a look at your
karma.

ROSIE: Back where?

MADAME CEUILI: Back THERE! The great beyond!

ROSIE: What's back there?

MADAME CEUILI: The Supreme Truth.

ROSIE: What about my two wishes? Can I still get my two
wishes?

MADAME CEUILI: This future business, everybody wants to
know. Will I get be happy, will I get a boyfriend. It sells big
but it don't teach nothing. Reincarnation is much better. Tells
us about the Soul.

ROSIE: The soul?

MADAME CEUILI: It is an ancient practice.

ROSIE: Have you ever tried it before?

MADAME CEUILI: You insult me, Lady. I am expert!

ROSIE: What would I have to do?

MADAME CEUILI: Return to the first Earth life relevant to the
one today and repeat the life-death cycle backward experienc-
ing as many incarnations as possible. Cross repeatedly back

and forth the chasm that separates birth and death to find your source.

ROSIE: Oy.

MADAME CEUILI: Your subconscious mind contains all memories of previous life. Human minds are like anchors that have lain too long on the ocean floor. They must be lifted out of muddy deception. We must search for THE GOLD. Every life that we encounter must increase our comprehension of ourselves as we are now. Attain the illumination. Follow the light. I will guide you on this journey by transferring my wisdom to your body with special techniques.

ROSIE: Like a mind meld?

MADAME CEUILI: This is not science fiction, Lady. This is supreme truth! Do or don't do. I could care less.

(MADAME CEUILI walks away from ROSIE to take a sip of her coffee.)

ROSIE: Does it hurt?

MADAME CEUILI: Every lifetime hurts a little bit. Some more than others.

ROSIE: Well . . . I have nowhere else to go this afternoon.

(ROSIE puts all her suicide tools away.)

MADAME CEUILI: OK!

ROSIE: OK!

(MADAME CEUILI blows out all the candles.)

MADAME CEUILI: Reincarnation Package Deluxe!

ROSIE *(Hopefully):* Reincarnation Package Deluxe!

MADAME CEUILI: Four lifetimes, seventy-five dollars.

ROSIE: Wait! Seventy-five MORE dollars?

MADAME CEUILI: Very draining. Much psychic energy. Extremely delicate work. To bring you back all in one piece.

ROSIE *(Overlapping):* Look, I don't have any credit cards. I already gave you everything I was supposed to spend on my phone bill and a new brassiere.

MADAME CEUILI: I tell you what. You in big trouble. Life is falling 'part. I make you a extra special deal. Mini deluxe. Three lives. No money down. *(Pause)* And your eyeglasses.

ROSIE: My eyeglasses? How am I going to see?

MADAME CEUILI: Maybe you see better after the reading. Never know. Anything could happen.

ROSIE *(Suspicious):* Why do you want my glasses?

MADAME CEUILI: To read! *People* magazine. *The Bible.* All them letter are so teeny weeny . . . can't see a fuckin' thing.

ROSIE: I must be nuts.

> *(ROSIE takes her glasses off and hands them to MADAME CEUILI. Pause. MADAME CEUILI puts ROSIE's glasses down and lifts up the crystal ball and chants.)*

MADAME CEUILI: Oh Cassandra! Guide me through the vale of darkness! Speak to me . . .

ROSIE *(Interrupting, overlapping):* What are you doing now?

MADAME CEUILI *(Overlapping):* SILENCE! Focus on the crystal. Never take your eyes off it. Keep your eyes open. Feet on the floor.

> *(MADAME CEUILI puts the crystal down in front of ROSIE. She closes her eyes. She begins swaying. She moves her hands in the air. ROSIE fidgets in her chair, crossing her legs.)*

MADAME CEUILI *(Eyes closed):* Feet on the floor!

> *(ROSIE puts both feet back on the floor. MADAME CEUILI is swaying and moving. ROSIE looks around the room.)*

MADAME CEUILI *(Eyes still closed):* Eyes on the crystal!

> *(ROSIE stares at the crystal ball. Strange music begins to play.)*

Time is flowing backward. See the road of living memory flowing from the center of self to the deepest heart of the crystal. A thin blue patch of mist. CONCENTRATE!

> *(Smoke comes up around the floor. Lights shift. Strange music gets louder. Blackout.)*

The Waiting Room

LISA LOOMER

The waiting room. Three chairs and a table with magazines. Boppy Muzak, preferably a Beatles tune. VICTORIA, a Victorian Englishwoman dressed in twenty pounds of clothes and tightly corseted, and FORGIVENESS FROM HEAVEN, in eighteenth-century Chinese robes . . . wait. After several moments of waiting, FORGIVENESS picks up Vogue. *She sniffs a perfume ad, delighted. VICTORIA picks up* Cosmo, *is horrified by the cover, and quickly puts it down. Finally, she takes a book from under her skirt and begins to read.*

FORGIVENESS: Pretty. Pretty, pretty . . . *(Shows VICTORIA the magazine)* Pretty, huh?
VICTORIA *(Politely):* Yes. *(She goes back to her book.)*
FORGIVENESS *(Eager to chat):* Long wait, huh?
VICTORIA: He's thorough.
    (A bloodcurdling scream offstage. The women barely react.)
FORGIVENESS: Good doctor.
VICTORIA: Oh yes.
    (FORGIVENESS smiles. VICTORIA remembers her manners.)
VICTORIA: Ah—Victoria Smoot.
FORGIVENESS: Forgiveness From Heaven.
VICTORIA: How do you do. *(She goes back to her book.)*
FORGIVENESS: Oh, fine. *(Smiles)* Little problem with little toe.
VICTORIA: Well, I'm sure the doctor will fix it.
FORGIVENESS: Fell off this morning.
VICTORIA: I'm so sorry. And your family? Your husband is well?
FORGIVENESS *(Smiles, covering pain):* With other wives this week.
VICTORIA: Nice for you . . . *(Sniffs)* By the way, do you smell something—untoward?

FORGIVENESS *(Proudly):* My feet!

VICTORIA: I beg your pardon?

FORGIVENESS: My feet. Stink bad, huh?

VICTORIA: No, no, not—too awfully.

FORGIVENESS: I would wash them, but my husband, he's crazy for the smell. Likes to eat watermelon seeds from the toes. Almonds. *(Delighted)* Dirt.

VICTORIA: Well . . . *(Searches, what can she say?)* I love your shoes. *(She goes back to her book.)*

FORGIVENESS: Size three.

VICTORIA: Three *inches?*

FORGIVENESS *(Competitive):* What size your waist?

VICTORIA: Sixteen! I got my first corset quite young.

FORGIVENESS: How young?

VICTORIA: Fourteen!

FORGIVENESS *(Tops her; shows feet):* I was five. *(Almost hopeful)* Corset hurts bad, huh?

VICTORIA: Oh, no. Only when I breathe.

FORGIVENESS: My feet, just first couple years.

VICTORIA: Really!

FORGIVENESS: My mother, you see—

VICTORIA *(Reflexively polite):* How is she?

FORGIVENESS: Oh, dead for long time now.

VICTORIA: Nice for her . . .

FORGIVENESS: One day mother say to me, "Forgiveness From Heaven, today is lucky day by moon. Time to start binding . . ."

VICTORIA: Ah.

FORGIVENESS *(Like a recipe):* Then mother takes bandage, place on inside of instep, and carry over small toes to force them in and toward the sole. Then bandage is wrapped around heel nice and forcefully, so heel and toes are drawn close, real close together.

VICTORIA: I see. *(Pause)* Why?

FORGIVENESS: Make feet pretty for future husband! *(Laughs)* That night, I tried to run away in the forest—my feet were on fire! But mother found me and forced me to walk. She was a good girl when her feet were bound and never cried.

VICTORIA *(Sighs):* And so your poor feet never grew. *(She goes back to her book.)*

FORGIVENESS: Got smaller! Soon the flesh became putrescent, and little pieces sloughed off from the sole as toes began to putrefy. *(Laughs)* When I ate salted fish, my feet would swell and pus would drip—oh terrible!

(VICTORIA gets up. Checks the clock. Circles the room. Anything.)

FORGIVENESS: Mother would remove bindings, lance corns with a needle, and wipe the pus and blood and dead flesh. . . . And every two weeks I changed shoes, each pair one quarter inch smaller.

(VICTORIA starts to gag and gets out her smelling salts.)

FORGIVENESS: And after two years my feet were practically dead—so no more pain! Finally, all the bones were broken and four toes bent in nice neat row toward plantar.

(VICTORIA falls back in her chair, faint.)

FORGIVENESS *(Triumphant):* And when I was nine, father betrothed me to my husband.

VICTORIA: Well. *(Pause)* I love your shoes. What time is your appointment for, by the way?

FORGIVENESS: Quarter past one. And yours?

VICTORIA: One fifteen.

(A scream offstage.)

FORGIVENESS: And what are *you* being treated for?

VICTORIA: Me? Oh . . . *(Yawns)* Hysteria.

FORGIVENESS: Hys—teria? *(She gets up and examines the rubber plant.)*

VICTORIA: It's a disease of the ovaries.

FORGIVENESS: Hurts bad, huh?

VICTORIA *(Condescending):* No, no, no. You see, the ovaries control the personality. I've done some reading on the matter. Though my husband says that reading makes me worse. Romantic novels especially. *(Proud)* My husband is a doctor.

(VICTORIA has a tic. Whenever she says the word "husband," her arm flings out from the waist, as if to swat someone.)

FORGIVENESS: Lucky. Has he treated you?

VICTORIA: Well, he did prescribe the rest cure.

FORGIVENESS: Nice and peaceful?

VICTORIA: Oh very. Six weeks on one's back in a dimly lit room. No reading, no visitors, no, ah . . . potty.

FORGIVENESS: Worked good?

VICTORIA: Well, I came out screaming, actually. But it was hardly my husband's fault. It seems—well, it seems, I've had too much education and my uterus has atrophied commensurately.

FORGIVENESS: Glad I never went to school.

VICTORIA: Lucky.

FORGIVENESS: When I was a little girl, my husband liked my little feet so much, I never left the bedroom.

VICTORIA: Well, children need rest.

FORGIVENESS: Men crazy for the golden lotus. Feel much love and pity for your suffering . . . the tiny steps, the whispered walk. *(Demonstrates)* And bound feet make buttocks larger, more attractive.

VICTORIA: Well, I assure you, it's a lot less fuss to wear a bustle.

FORGIVENESS: Bustle? Not natural! Also, foot binding makes vagina tighter.

(VICTORIA has another tic. Sex makes her nose twitch.)

FORGIVENESS: When I walk, whole lower part of my body is in a state of tension, so vagina becomes like little fist!

VICTORIA *(After a beat):* Mrs. From Heaven, do you know erotic tendencies are one of the primary symptoms of ovarian disease—

FORGIVENESS *(Worried):* Erotic tendencies are . . . ?

VICTORIA: Obviously you do not keep abreast of modern science.

FORGIVENESS: But what if husband *insists* on erotic tendencies?

VICTORIA: Well, that's not your "tendency," dear, that's your *duty. (Leans in)* And need we mention the perils of the ah . . . well, the, ah . . .vice?

FORGIVENESS: The vice?

VICTORIA: Leads to lesions, TB, dementia—I strap the children's hands down every night!

(A scream offstage.)

VICTORIA: And catch it early because clitorectomy and cauterization can be quite costly.

FORGIVENESS *(Scared):* This—vice—can cause disease in grown women too?

VICTORIA: Mrs. From Heaven. There are even *some* women who become enthralled by the stimulation of gynecological instruments!— *(Twitching and insinuating)* begging every doctor to institute an examination of the, ah—the ah, sexual ah—

FORGIVENESS: Wait just a minute, Mrs. Smoot. *(Huffy)* I'm only here to have toe put back! Only here for that reason!

VICTORIA: Well! I'm just here to see about removing the ovaries!

(WANDA, forty, a modern gal from New Jersey, enters in an outfit that pays homage to her enormous breasts. She carries a back-breaking pocketbook and a clipboard with her chart, and takes the empty seat between them.)

WANDA: Excuse me, you reading that *Cosmo*?

VICTORIA: Take it!

FORGIVENESS: *Two* ovaries? *(As VICTORIA speaks, WANDA is distracted by VICTORIA's story.)*

VICTORIA *(With mounting hysteria):* Well, we've tried everything else! Injections to the womb—water, milk, tea, a decoction of marshmallow. I've stopped reading and writing, stopped stimulating my emotions with operas and French plays. Last week the doctor placed leeches on my vulva—

(WANDA's mouth falls open. She gets out her cigarettes.)

VICTORIA: Some were quite adventurous, actually, and traveled all the way to the cervical cavity! The pressure from the corset's forcing my uterus out through my vagina. . . . And according to my husband, my hysteria's only getting worse! My husband says I've all the classic symptoms of ovarian disease: troublesomeness, eating like a ploughman, painful menstruation—a desire to learn Greek! Attempted suicide, persecution mania, and simple cussedness! Last night I sneezed continuously for twenty-seven minutes, and tried to *bite* my own husband! What can I do? I shan't be beaten across the face and body with wet towels like an Irish woman—I JUST WANT THE DAMN THINGS OUT!

WANDA *(After a beat):* Just the way I feel about my tits.

The Soprano's Dinner
from *Dream of a Common Language*

HEATHER MCDONALD

A garden behind a French Country House. Inside the house, a group of painters, all male, gather for a dinner to plan the first Impressionist exhibit. Outside the house, in the garden, are the three women. They have been excluded from the dinner, so they organize their own alternative dinner, The Soprano's Dinner. All are in their mid thirties. CLOVIS stopped painting a year earlier. She is mother to nine-year-old Mylo. POLA is also a painter, although in a different style, and an old friend. She travels a lot and alone. DOLORES is also on her own and lives as a companion to the family. They've all had a bit to drink.

DOLORES *(Entering):* More wine, a bowl for the berries, and glazed carrots.

POLA: Bravo, Dolores. Brava.

> *(CLOVIS enters.)*

CLOVIS: Chicken legs! I've got chicken legs!

POLA: Oh, this is wonderful.

DOLORES: Candles and berries and Mandarin oranges. Oh, it's a many-colored dinner.

> *(The women finish arranging their dinner and sit round the table.)*

CLOVIS *(A toast):* I officially announce the beginning of The Soprano's Dinner.

POLA & DOLORES: The Soprano's Dinner.

> *(They drink a toast.)*

DOLORES: And for hors d'oeuvres . . .

> *(DOLORES pulls out her bag of candies.)*

POLA: Hundreds and Thousands Candies!

DOLORES: It was the Hundreds and Thousands that taught me

how to live. Tiny things that add up. Too insignificant to be considered individually, but a handful of these candies lapped up and sticking to my tongue made me feel very full. And like these candies, the little scraps of my life have added up and made a definite pattern. Thank you tiny Hundreds and Thousands.

POLA & CLOVIS: Thank you, tiny Hundreds and Thousands.
   (The women dig in.)

CLOVIS: I used to lie awake at night waiting for the dawn to come so that I could start working. I used to sing while I worked, and people would ask, are you really that happy?

POLA: And were you?

CLOVIS: I was. I really was that happy.

DOLORES: I am happy eating chicken legs with whipped cream.

POLA: So am I.

CLOVIS: One day I was painting. It was late afternoon. I was alone, completely alone, and there was this moment when I knew I was finished and I stepped back and drank a glass of water, and I looked at what I had done and it was good. And there I was all alone, no one to share the moment with, but I didn't care because I knew that I had made something good. Then Victor came in and said, "When are you going to finish it?"

POLA: Why did you marry Victor straight out of the Academy?

CLOVIS: The minute I heard my first love story, I started looking. *(DOLORES smiles.)*

POLA: Why didn't you test other possibilities?

DOLORES: Women have always made bargains to avoid aloneness.

POLA: At least you have that, a marriage. Always, after leaving somebody, a group, a party, any situation where I have been included in the lives of others, my singleness impinges on me and I think, here we are, Pola, alone again.

CLOVIS: Marriage can be lonelier than solitude.

POLA: Yes, I suppose it can.

CLOVIS: It is a cushion, but you are still alone. You still have to make your life.

DOLORES: I know how you felt when you finished that painting. Many years ago I lived in a village called Medjugorge. In late February all the women go into the church to celebrate the rites of spring. We sing. We dance. We run naked through the woods to a stream, jump in the freezing water and run back through the woods, wet, naked, holding hands and laughing. Oh, the laughter of those women ringing through the woods.

CLOVIS: Let's make a list of all the women we know who are doing well.

(Long pause)

POLA: There's Elise.

CLOVIS: Elise pushed her husband down a flight of stairs.

POLA: Oh. *(Small giggle)* Is he all right?

DOLORES *(A giggle):* No, he's not.

CLOVIS: What about Clothilde?

POLA: She has to wear a brace for her spine.

(More giggles)

DOLORES: What about that woman Lucille?

CLOVIS: She abandoned her husband and children and went to live in a nunnery.

(The women are laughing by now.)

POLA: All right, all right, I've got one. Marie-Louise.

CLOVIS: Have you seen Marie-Louise in the last year?

POLA: No.

CLOVIS: She has developed an odd facial tic. *(Clovis demonstrates the tic. Howls.)*

POLA: There has to be someone.

CLOVIS: There's you, Pola.

POLA: Me?

CLOVIS: We could write your name on our list of women who are doing well.

POLA: I don't think so.

DOLORES: You travel.

CLOVIS: You know interesting people.

DOLORES: You have adventures.

CLOVIS: You have a rich life, Pola.

POLA: I have a bicycle and I roam from place to place.

CLOVIS: Why did you start traveling?

POLA: Because of Madeleine.

CLOVIS: She was so beautiful.

POLA: And so much more than Tissot's mistress.

DOLORES: If I ever have a daughter, I will wish for one who is beautiful and stupid.

POLA: She was lover, cook, bookkeeper, student, model, muse, assistant. He chucked her out, so she went around scratching her name into his pieces right next to his. She hadn't come from much so had nothing to return to. She roamed the streets stopping people to tell them, "I did the hands and feet." They kept denying her. You see, they could not believe she was so good. And Tissot is known especially for his hands and feet. So in the end, he had her put away, and her name was rubbed off the statues. *(Beat)* I went to visit her in the sanatorium. We sat in the sun eating biscuits and I said to her, "Madeleine, we're close friends, tell me the truth about those hands and feet." I have never forgiven myself for that. *(Beat)* Shortly after that afternoon of eating biscuits in the sun, she hung herself from a hook in her closet.

DOLORES: You can't blame yourself.

POLA: There was a nun at the sanatorium who had secretly been supplying Madeleine with clay and wet cloths, and when they found her hanging in the closet, they also found dozens of the most beautifully molded clay hands and feet wrapped in white sheets. Every one was signed and dated. *(Beat)* Not long after that I went away.

CLOVIS: But why did you stop painting?

POLA: Because secretly, somewhere deep down inside of me, I realized that I honestly didn't believe we were as good as they were. That we could ever be as good. Remember how I was always the one shouting the loudest about being allowed into the art schools, being able to come to life class? In those days, I was always shouting. But part of me believed that I would never be as good as Victor, as good as Marc. And when I saw work that was good, really good, I couldn't believe that a woman had done it.

CLOVIS: So you stopped painting.

POLA: Yes, for a year.

DOLORES: But you started again.

CLOVIS: Whatever it was that happened to you, you eventually did start painting again.

POLA: Something beautiful fooled me into it. I was in the jungle looking for the night moonflower. They're rare and only open at night when the moon is full. I wanted to see one, so night after night I sat in the jungle waiting. One night the moonflower opened. Without thinking, I took out a scrap of paper and a pencil and I drew. I began drawing again. For me. I went into town the next day and bought a crude set of children's watercolors and began painting flowers and plants and insects. For me.

CLOVIS: Dolores, do you remember a time when you were doing well?

DOLORES: All of my most intense memories go back to child-hood.

CLOVIS: Mine, too.

POLA: Mine, too.

CLOVIS: In childhood, then, do you remember a time when you felt clear about who you were and your place in the world?

DOLORES: When I was eleven.

CLOVIS: What happened then?

DOLORES: I remember that when people would tell me things that didn't seem right or true, I was very clear about saying, "No, that's not right, that's not true."

POLA: When I was eleven, I remember seeing everything with such particular clarity. Colors were brighter. Lines were sharper. I remember thinking, I need to notice this because a lot is going to be expected of me.

CLOVIS: When I was eleven, my father showed me a room made of glass, and I was surrounded by light.

POLA: When I was eleven, I asked my great Aunt Elise, "Am I pretty?" She said, "Develop your brain and an interesting character."

DOLORES: When I was eleven, my father left me with Challah Borovsky who taught me to tell fortunes.

CLOVIS: Papa?

DOLORES: My mother was beautiful.

CLOVIS: My mother was beautiful.

POLA: I can't remember my mother.

DOLORES: I wasn't beautiful.

POLA: Oh, I was never pretty.

CLOVIS: I was always pretty.

DOLORES: I couldn't do tricks, ride bareback, walk on my hands, or juggle.

CLOVIS: Right, Papa?

POLA: I developed my brain.

DOLORES: How could they take me with them?

POLA: How could he take me with him?

DOLORES: I couldn't even juggle.

POLA: So off I went.

DOLORES: So off I went to Challah Borovsky's.

CLOVIS: The Revolution was awful, wasn't it, Papa? I like this scarf, don't you, Papa?

DOLORES: I remember my mother and father riding two beautiful white barebacked horses.

CLOVIS: Red wine is better than white, isn't it, Papa?

POLA: I won't apologize for who I am.

DOLORES: Gold ribbons fly behind them.

POLA: So off I went to Java to see a shadow play and to climb the Borobodur. I wore saffron-colored trousers, a purple turban, and carried a walking stick.

DOLORES: And they were laughing.

CLOVIS: This is beautiful.

POLA: They'd never seen a woman in saffron-colored trousers atop the Borobodur.

CLOVIS: I was surrounded by the most extraordinary smell. Cinnamon.

POLA: What lengths to go for a chance at joy.

CLOVIS: Astonishing.

POLA: And oh how marvelous.

CLOVIS: That girl was me. Oh, let's go back, let's go back to being eleven-year-old girls.

POLA: God, yes, let's be eleven again. Eleven-year-old girls with clear blue eyes.

DOLORES: Mine are brown.

POLA: Dolores, when you were eleven, did you have a favorite game?

DOLORES: King Dido Died.

CLOVIS: King Dido Died?

DOLORES: You don't know King Dido Died?

POLA: We don't know King Dido Died.

DOLORES: You poor deprived children. First you march around in a circle. *(The women march in a circle.)* Then you chant. *(POLA and CLOVIS follow DOLORES.)* King Dido, King Dido, King Dido died, *(Clap, clap)* King Dido died, *(Clap, clap)* King Dido died doing this. *(And DOLORES flaps one arm and shakes her hips back and forth in a wild fashion.)* King Dido, King Dido. Pola. *(And POLA leads the chant.)*

POLA: King Dido, King Dido, King Dido died, *(Clap, clap)* King Dido died, *(Clap, clap)* King Dido died doing this. *(And she imitates DOLORES, one arm flapping and hips shaking and she adds something of her own.)* King Dido, King Dido. Clovis.

CLOVIS: King Dido, King Dido, King Dido died, *(Clap, clap)* King Dido died, *(Clap, clap)* King Dido died doing this.

(CLOVIS imitates DOLORES's actions and then POLA's and then adds her own movements. The women continue the game, repeating the chant and growing wilder and freer. King Dido builds and builds as the women create a kind of pagan dance. Finally, the game peaks and they collapse breathless.)

DOLORES: A falling star.

POLA: Oh, god, make a wish.

CLOVIS: Make wishes for us all.

(The women stop and look up and each silently makes a wish.)

Mothers

KATHLEEN MCGHEE-ANDERSON

MARIKO, a Japanese American, has moved to the United States after marrying an African American soldier. In her new country, she is alienated from both the Japanese and African American communities. Into the Southside Chicago apartment building that MARIKO manages moves JEAN, a white Kentuckian who has also married a black male and is ostracized by both family and community. Both women, now divorced, struggle to raise their mixed-race, teenage daughters. Alone and alienated, MARIKO returns to Chicago after visiting Tokyo to bury her grandmother, only to find that her daughter has run away.

MARIKO *(Entering apartment):* Tami! *(MARIKO reopens the door to her apartment, comes back out.)* Have you seen my daughter?

JEAN: I haven't. *(MARIKO leans against the door of her apartment. Her eyes glaze over. She goes far away.)* You OK? *(MARIKO begins sinking in her doorwell. Getting closer and closer to the ground.)*

MARIKO: Grandmother is gone. Tamiko is gone. I have nothing to live for.

JEAN *(Nervously):* Why don't I help you into your place?
> *(JEAN crosses to MARIKO, puts her arm around her. MARIKO collapses against her.)*

MARIKO: I want to die! *(JEAN guides MARIKO back into her apartment.)* I have brought shame and dishonor upon my family.
> *(JEAN lowers MARIKO into a chair. Begins to remove her coat and hat.)*

JEAN: Whatever you did it can't be worse than me.

MARIKO: I married out of my race. I bore a child that disgraced my family.

JEAN: You're not to blame.

MARIKO: I am nothing. Not Japanese. Not American. Not Negro. Not white. I'm not even a woman anymore.

JEAN *(Interrupting):* Hey wait a minute. I know what they've done to you. But I'll be damned if I'll let them take my sex away from me. They can take away everything else. My home. My family. My race. But they can't fuck with my vagina!

MARIKO: Look at my hands. My hands are rough. My feet are the feet of a man's.

JEAN: Who says?

MARIKO: I've walked this ground too long.

(JEAN crosses to the sink, runs water in a bucket.)

JEAN: Don't let their dirt sink beneath the skin. You've just got to keep scrubbing it off— *(JEAN carries the bucket over to MARIKO, takes her shoes off, puts her feet in the water, and begins to bathe them tenderly.)* —rubbing it off, rinsing it away.

(There is silence. The sound of the water, wind, a distant chime. MARIKO releases.)

MARIKO: It's been so long . . .

JEAN: Since anyone's heard you?

MARIKO: Since I've had anyone to talk to.

JEAN: I know.

MARIKO: Since anyone's touched me.

JEAN: Tell me about it.

MARIKO: Since anyone even cared. *(JEAN carefully takes her feet out of the water.)* Thank you. *(JEAN pats her feet dry.)* Thank you for being here.

JEAN: If it makes you feel any better my daughter's gone, too. *(Beat)* Both of them.

(MARIKO rises to comfort JEAN.)

MARIKO: I'm sorry, I really am. *(Beat)* I could use a drink. I bet you could, too. *(JEAN sits, nods. The weight of her situation descending.)* What happened?

JEAN: Donna went back to Vegas. Penny ran away. *(MARIKO goes into her suitcase and unwraps two sake glasses. She pours wine. JEAN speaks to keep from crying.)* These are pretty.

MARIKO: My grandmother's glasses.

JEAN: A lady I clean for has some like these.

(MARIKO hands JEAN a glass. They drink.)

MARIKO: I brought back her plum wine from Tokyo, and her silk kimonos. One of them for Tami to get married in.

(MARIKO takes a beautiful white kimono from the suitcase and admires it.)

JEAN: You were in Tokyo?

MARIKO: My grandmother died.

JEAN: That's too bad. *(They sit awkwardly for a few seconds, sipping the wine.)* I'm sorry to hear that. *(MARIKO puts the kimono back in the suitcase and closes it, as if shutting away memories. She pours more wine.)* I pray to God Penny's not living in a cardboard box, or in the backseat of a car.

MARIKO: I'll forgive Tami anything, just as long as she's not with that man she was seeing.

JEAN: What man?

(MARIKO downs the glass, pours more.)

MARIKO: No-good, uneducated bum she met on the street. I'm thinking about joining the police force just so I can track his butt down.

JEAN: You go for those jobs where you wear a badge, huh?

MARIKO: Hell no. But city jobs pay benefits. Better than those jobs where you wear an apron and opaque stockings.

JEAN: The tips are good.

(JEAN reaches over and pours more wine. They are beginning to get tipsy.)

MARIKO: You know, ever since you moved here, I couldn't stand you.

JEAN: Same here.

MARIKO: I never in my whole life saw a white woman as pitiful as you. There is no excuse for you to be doing as bad as you are. It makes me disgusted.

JEAN: And you don't have a clue, you know that? Running around thinking you're going places and you're just taking one step forward and two steps back. If you weren't such a joke, you'd disgust me, too.

(They sit considering what's been said.)

MARIKO *(Agreeing with her):* I don't even have a job.

JEAN: Neither do I.

MARIKO: A man held me up in the subway. Took my purse, all the city's money, everything. I quit that night.

JEAN: I got sick of my boss hassling me about Penny. So I told him where he could go, switched the pancake batter and the fried fish grease, dumped the roach motels on the floor, and called the Health Department over to inspect him.

MARIKO: What are you going to do now?

JEAN: I don't know. I've been looking for another job. What about you?

MARIKO: A guy I know owns a gas station. Maybe I'll pump gas.

JEAN: There you go. Another uniform. Got the badge sewn on it too.

MARIKO: He's kind of cute. Said the sole of my foot looks better than most women's face.

JEAN: I don't have time for that simple mess.

MARIKO: You look like you haven't had a man since Penny was born.

JEAN: I'm not into being a one-night stand. Guys see Penny and think I'm a big-time freak.

MARIKO: They don't even have to see Tami. They look at me and get ready for sex-kink from the Orient.

JEAN: We fucked up, didn't we?

MARIKO: Yeah. I can't stand white people for doing me this way.

JEAN: Neither can I. But my in-laws were pretty disgusting, too. They were about as black as this painted cup.

MARIKO: Lacquer. Colored folks are as pitiful as they want to be.

JEAN: Yeah, we got it bad. But at least we ain't colored.

MARIKO: Some days I have to look in the mirror though. Make sure I'm still Mariko.

JEAN: Naw, you ain't colored yet.

MARIKO: Neither are you. But you don't look all that white anymore either.

JEAN: It's 'cause I don't use hairspray. White folks use hairspray. *(JEAN stands. She has to steady herself.)* You want to come over to my apartment for some dinner?

MARIKO: What are you fixing?

JEAN: Greens and corn bread.

MARIKO: You put fatback in the greens?

JEAN: Salt pork.

MARIKO: Umph, umph, umph! Sounds good to me.

(JEAN reaches into MARIKO's open suitcase and removes a jar of pickled eel.)

JEAN: What's this?

MARIKO: Pickled eel.

JEAN: Bring that too, and some more of that wine if you have it. We might as well have us a party.

MARIKO *(Standing):* Long as you don't play that loud-ass country-sounding music.

JEAN: I told you those records weren't mine. They belonged to my daughter.

MARIKO: Which one?

JEAN: The white one.

MARIKO: First you had one, then you had two, now you got none.

JEAN: Being a mother sure is a bitch.

MARIKO: You got that right.

(They start to the door and have to hold each other up. They exit.)

Tripping Through the Car House

REGINA PORTER

NITA, alone in the house, takes advantage of the space to smoke a cigarette. Her sister, BERYL, enters from outside.

BERYL: Boo!

NITA *(Jumps):* Jesus. Big Beryl—that is not funny!

BERYL: You saw the way your eyes nearly popped out of your head, you wouldn't be saying that.

NITA: Shouldn't you be at work?

BERYL: I quit.

NITA: Really?

> *(Pause)*

BERYL: Well, actually, I was fired. Truth is, I'm glad to be fired.

NITA: What they fire you for this time?

BERYL: Customer's always right. I just don't seem to know it . . .

NITA: Uh huh?

BERYL: I'm fixing this customer's hair a certain way like she asked me to. And then she says she don't like her hair that way. And I say, "Honey, then why did you ask for that style in the first place? I told you it wasn't gonna work. You got one of those big pie faces. Don't necessarily do well with that style." And before you know it, who's complaining—who's saying, "Your girl's telling me I got a pie face. I do not have a pie face. Everybody knows I got an oval face. A tiny oval face. And even in case I don't, which I do, she still didn't fix my hair right like I asked her." "But it's like you asked me." "No, it ain't." "Yes, it is." Manager says, "Now, Big Beryl, the customer is always right. Apologize. Tell the customer she's right." And I say, "If I do, a monkey'll jump out of a rabbit's ass." And everybody knows, a monkey can't do that, which means the end of me.

NITA: You know Mama's gonna find out.

BERYL: I'm a good beautician. Good beauticians can always find jobs. *(Looking around)* Where is she anyway?

NITA: Last minute grocery shopping for your "fiancé."

(BERYL moves over to the dinner table, which is already set.)

BERYL: Do not call him that.

NITA: I'm just telling you what Mama's been telling her sewing customers. She swears you've found the one.

(BERYL puts out NITA's cigarette.)

BERYL: Y'all know more about my personal life than I do.

NITA: The one.

BERYL: Nita, a little quiet. Quiet, please. *(Pause)* I got some headache.

NITA: Want me to massage it for you?

BERYL: Would you? Would you be a dear?

NITA: I won't be "a dear" but I'll massage it for you, if you'd like.

BERYL: I'd like.

(BERYL sits. NITA massages her head.)

NITA: How does that feel?

BERYL: Good.

NITA: Good as when Frazier kisses you?

BERYL: Not quite that good.

NITA: So, he has kissed you.

BERYL: Of course.

NITA: How many times?

BERYL: I've lost count.

NITA: That many times?

BERYL: Girl, it's no big deal.

NITA: But if it wasn't a big deal—he wouldn't have kissed you so many times you've lost count. It's a very big deal. Why, Big Beryl, sometimes at night, I sit up and lift my arm like this— *(She lifts her arm toward her.)* And I kiss it just as long and hard as I can. I imagine it's Mr. Clint Eastwood done stepped

118

out of his poster world right smack into mine. He pulls me all up next to him—so real close next to him—that my body just generates all of this— this—

BERYL: Heat.

NITA: And I say, "Mr. Clint Eastwood, tomorrow you're gonna be having yourself a big old showdown with Mr. Lee Van Cleef." And he says *(Imitates Eastwood),* "I know." *(Back to her own voice)* And I say, "If you're gonna be having such a big old showdown with Mr. Lee Van Cleef, you're gonna need your rest." And he says *(Imitates Eastwood),* "A man gets by in life on his ability to rest." *(Her own voice)* And I say, "Lay alongside my pillow here for a little while? Rest a spell." And he says *(Imitates Eastwood),* "Alright, Nita. Alright."

BERYL: Girl, you need to take that Clint Eastwood poster off your wall.

NITA: Yeah—right.

BERYL: You need to take it off and look at someone else—a boy in this neighborhood. Preacherboyson even.

NITA: I look at Preacherboyson every day.

BERYL: That's my point. Why spend all your time imagining when you can have the real thing?

NITA: Preacherboyson and Mr. Clint Eastwood ain't in the same league.

BERYL: Neither is "Mr. Clint Eastwood" and you.

NITA: You saying he wouldn't like me, Big Beryl?

BERYL: I'm saying little things lead to big things. Big things lead to cruel realities. And one cruel reality, Nita, is that little black girls don't fit squarely into the lives of the Mr. Clint Eastwoods of this world. Peripherally: yes. Sometimes. Some ways. But squarely: no.

NITA: I don't believe you, Big Beryl.

BERYL: Believe what you want.

Designed for Sacrifice

PATRICIA S. SMITH

LILA prided herself on being a model wife—compliant, immaculate, gracious. And so she was stunned when after twenty years of marriage, her husband, a well-known Chevy Chase architect, said he was leaving her and taking with him the house she had spent ten years designing, a magnificent piece of architecture that she assumed they would be moving into together within the next few weeks. In the habit of behaving perfectly, LILA has no skills with which to defend herself or her property. Her neighbors, including BETTY, one of the world's consummate caregivers, and CHERYL, a tough professional, convince her to begin therapy immediately.

On a crash course to find out why she is so paralyzed, LILA reenters lives lived over millennia as sacrificer and sacrificee, betrayer and betrayed. As LILA's personality metamorphoses beyond the reaches of suburban perfection, the pull is irresistible to BETTY and CHERYL, who become enmeshed in secrets of lives past but not forgotten.

LILA's living room, morning. The room features a large aquarium filled with fish swimming in a sea of nonfish food. LILA is asleep on the sofa. She is in Egyptian makeup. She is wearing a robe and has a gold scarf tied around her head. LILA wakes in fits and starts, sees her clothes, touches her face, hurries to the mirror.

LILA: Omigod! *(She looks at herself in the mirror from different angles.)* So, perfect wife, what do you think now? *(She strikes different poses in the mirror.)* Maybe one of those cobra heads. *(She puts her hand in a cobra head position at her forehead. The doorbell rings.* LILA *is startled. She looks at the clock that says the time is slightly after 9:00 A.M.)* Shit. *(To the fish)* Don't just keep swimming, do something.

BETTY *(From outside):* Lila, it's me, Betty. Are you in there?

LILA *(Touching her body):* My god, how could I possibly tell?

BETTY: I made a little cake.

LILA: "Chevy Chase matron goes berserk. Dressed as an Egyptian, Lila Sayor, wife of one of our nation's leading architects, murdered the family fish. 'Let them eat cake,' she said."

    (The doorbell rings again.)

LILA: I'm coming!

BETTY: It's just a little chocolate sour cream cake.

    (LILA opens the door with a flourish.)

Oh, I'm so glad you're up. I just made this little cake and thought I'd *(She is momentarily stopped as she realizes LILA is in costume.)* run it over before the girls . . . while the girls, ah, . . . are at nursery school.

    (She hands LILA the cake.)

LILA *(Overly elegant):* Oh, it is beautiful!

    (BETTY stares at LILA as she walks in.)

BETTY: Are you . . . ? How are you?

LILA *(Effervescent):* I'm great! I'm just great!

BETTY *(Still staring):* It's been hard getting hold of you.

LILA: I'm not answering the phone.

BETTY: Yes. . . . Actually Cheryl said that. . . . *(Continuing brightly)* But I did try.

LILA *(Continuing graciously):* I know, I heard you on the machine.

BETTY: Yes, . . . well, ah, . . . I was just making a little something for the recycling options bake-off. I don't even know if you like chocolate sour cream cake, but there I was anyway, so . . . here it is. Do you like chocolate sour cream cake?

LILA: Betty, you are the best human being on the planet.

BETTY: I don't know about that. Between the girls and Ralph . . . and now the recycling committee. Sometimes I just feel overwhelmed.

LILA: You must. Recycling by itself is a big job.

BETTY: I didn't know you were interested in recycling.

LILA: Me? I'm a convert.

BETTY: You think you know someone and then a whole new part pops up.

LILA: Isn't that true? . . . *(She turns in a direct frontal position towards BETTY.)* What do you think about my new look? Are the brows a little heavy?

BETTY: You're trying new makeup. Lila, is my cake ill-timed?

LILA: I'm sure it's perfect. Your cooking is fabulous.

BETTY: I didn't mean that.

LILA: Is your visit propitious?

BETTY: That's what I meant.

LILA: I spent the night on the sofa as a pair of incestuous Egyptian twins who design pyramids. But other than that, your timing is perfect.

BETTY *(Without missing a beat):* Do you feel better now?

LILA *(Amused and surprised):* Why, yes, I think I do. That was very good, Betty.

BETTY: Thank you. Lila, did something happen at the doctor's?

LILA: Have you ever been in love with yourself?

BETTY: Do I like myself?

LILA: No, not do you *like* yourself. Do you *lust* yourself?

BETTY: I suspect the more esoteric joys have not yet come my way. Is that why you have on so much makeup, Lil'? Have you fallen in love with yourself?

LILA: It's lust.

BETTY: Lust.

LILA: What do you think of my robe?

BETTY: Gold looks good on you.

LILA: You noticed! Betty! You are doing extremely well!

BETTY: I am?

LILA: I must say I'm surprised.

BETTY: So am I.

LILA: OK, are you ready?

BETTY: Sure.

LILA: Have you noticed I am undergoing a personality change?

BETTY: You're acting a little different.

LILA: Eh, eh, eh.

BETTY: I think you've gone off the wall.

LILA *(Buoyant):* Right!

BETTY: I'm here to help you.

LILA *(A tad malicious):* Whoops, down one. "Bleep" on Betty.
    (LILA turns her back to BETTY.)

BETTY: I didn't mean to upset you.

LILA *(Ignoring her):* But you came to check me out, didn't you?

BETTY: Lila, you're not answering the phone. We're worried.

LILA: I bet.

BETTY *(Apologetically, but going forward):* Cheryl said you two
    made laurels because you were . . . "technically" sacrificed . . .
    at Stonehenge or some place like that.

LILA *(Angry):* It wasn't Stonehenge.

BETTY: Not exactly, but . . .

LILA *(Angry):* Not even inexactly. Stonehenge is obvious.
    Stonehenge can be found in the books. Everyone knows where
    Stonehenge is. There's a major highway by it, for god's sake.
    Where I was was just a little valley. It can't be found in books. I
    was the Celtics. Heard of them? They didn't have time to pull
    big rocks hundreds of miles just to show off. Life was rough.
    I'm basic. I'm "*pre*" everything! There's nothing artsy left for a
    bunch of tourists to gawk at. I was just a valley and the . . .
    wind . . . and . . . the wind finally . . . and sun . . . and . . .
    (Pause)

BETTY: It sounds lovely.

LILA: Unfortunately they thought little girls were for offerings.

BETTY: That's what Cheryl said.

LILA *(With disdain):* So I'm to be tended by the two of you?

BETTY: Cheryl said she thought you were fine but that we
    should . . .

LILA: Well, I'm not a sheep and you don't get to be my watch-
    dog.

BETTY *(Tough):* Caring for you does not make me a watchdog.

(Pause)

LILA *(Quietly):* I killed people.

BETTY *(Amazed, quiet):* You *killed* people?!

LILA *(Sober):* I'm sorry.

BETTY: Don't be sorry to me!

LILA: I'm not being easy.

BETTY: Listen, I've got the morning. The girls are at school. I made a cake. . . . *(Deep breath)* So . . . who is the Egyptian?

LILA: Egypt*ians.*

BETTY *(Slightly squeamish):* Right. Incest. I forgot.

LILA: Of course you did.

BETTY *(Piqued):* Lil', if you want me to go away, I'll go away.

LILA: No! I mean, god, you come in here like a Samaritan sheep-dog . . .

BETTY: I'm sorry.

LILA: . . . convince me I need tending, and then say you're going away.

BETTY: I didn't say that.

LILA: If you want to help, you gotta stick around a couple minutes, okay? It was only a little incest.

BETTY: I'm here.

LILA *(Slightly panicked):* Good. This is heavy stuff I'm going through.

BETTY: I'm here.

LILA: Well, good.

BETTY: I said I was here.

LILA: Good.

BETTY: Good.

LILA: Fine.

BETTY: Fine.

LILA: Let's have cake.

BETTY: Good.

LILA: We did that part. Do you think Cleopatra would like cake?

BETTY: You were Cleopatra's incestuous twin!?

LILA: Betty, you are a life-giving force unto yourself. I adore you.

BETTY *(Blurts out):* But Cheryl is right, you have changed.

LILA *(Stricken):* Ouch.

BETTY: Oh, god, now I've done it. I'm so sorry.

LILA: It was just a . . . ouch! . . . wave of pain. . . . *(She clutches her chest.)*

BETTY *(Frustrated):* Sometimes I just say things and they hurt people and all I'm trying to do is just say things.

LILA *(Having trouble speaking):* That's probably a common problem for saints.

BETTY: What can I do?

LILA: Get plates.

BETTY: Now?!

LILA: They're above Mr. Coffee, forks beneath. . . . *(She nods without removing her arms from her chest.)*

BETTY *(Getting plates and forks):* This is terrible.

LILA: Oh, it's nothing compared to the Egyptians.

BETTY: Here you're trying to process everything, and I blurt out some stupid . . .

LILA: It's *fine*, Betty!

BETTY: I want to help!

LILA: I'm trying to get beyond that.

BETTY: Oh, god. I am so . . . What am I?

LILA: Solicitous, over attentive, and chronically apologetic.

BETTY: I'm sorry.

LILA: Betty . . .

BETTY: I've got to change. I've just got to. I can't go on this way.

LILA: . . . you make a great cake.

BETTY: Does that count?

LILA: Immensely. Napkins in the drawer next to the silver.

BETTY *(Getting the napkins):* But you *have* changed, Lil', you really *have*.

LILA: I know. And after we eat cake, I plan to talk about slaves and death.

BETTY: Oh, that's so much better.

LILA *(Progressively more subdued):* Does the living room have any hope of a clean surface?

BETTY: I think so. . . . *(She starts to clear the coffee table.)*

LILA *(Still holding her sides):* You haven't said anything about my housekeeping.

BETTY: Cheryl warned me.

LILA: Did she tell you how bad the fish tank was?

BETTY: Just a couple watchdogs. Arf, arf. . . . *(BETTY returns to the kitchen with old coffee cups.)*

LILA: I never knew you were funny.

BETTY: "Ha, ha"?

LILA: Unhuh. . . . *(Continues to hold her chest.)* I hurt.

BETTY: I can tell.

LILA: Will you want coffee?

BETTY: This cake doesn't need coffee.

LILA: Come. . . . *(She puts her arm through BETTY's. They carry plates of cake.)*

BETTY: It's good cake.

> *(LILA looks at BETTY in surprise.)*

LILA: Of course it is.

Strains of Papa's Violin

ARLENE STERNE

It is late evening, January 1982, and LAURA FLANNIGAN and her nineteen-year-old daughter, BONNIE, are straightening up the living room of their suburban home outside of Boston. Aunt Hannah, who has traveled from England to be reunited with her sister, LAURA, after a forty-year separation, is asleep upstairs. The two have not seen each other since LAURA, an aspiring violinist, was sent to America as a child to escape the Nazi terror. Now the owner of a posh art gallery and a pillar of the community, LAURA has forged a new identity and converted to a new religion in order to hide a traumatic past.

BONNIE: Poor Aunt Hannah! I never saw anyone konk out so fast.

LAURA: Don't forget, she's six hours ahead.

BONNIE: It must be hard for her.

LAURA: It wasn't exactly easy for me.

BONNIE: You think it was easy for me when I told Nelson we were Jewish?

LAURA: What did he say?

BONNIE: Mom, it doesn't matter what other people say. Why should you care? I think it's a sensation! I mean . . . two sisters meeting after forty years? *(Pause)* Maybe you shouldn't have been so . . . so blunt with her. Poor Aunt Hannah! She was so bummed!

LAURA: Hey, I'm not the first convert she's met.

BONNIE: But you're her sister. Put yourself in her shoes. I mean . . . you rejected your parents. Right?

LAURA: You're putting words in my mouth again.

BONNIE: I mean . . . they're *her* parents. *My* grandparents. It's like . . . you're creating a . . . Holocaust . . . in your own family. . . .

LAURA: What are you getting at? What kind of talk is this?

BONNIE: Isn't that what Hitler wanted? To wipe the Jews off the face of the earth?

LAURA: Are you comparing me with Hitler?

BONNIE: Sorry. I didn't mean it that way. *(Beat)* Poor Hannah! She was in shock when she went upstairs. She went right to her room and shut the door.

LAURA: So what do I do? Give up my religion to please my sister?

BONNIE: Just accept who you are. That's all.

LAURA: Look, let's get this straight. This is *my* problem. Not yours!

BONNIE: My God, Mother! They were *my* family, too!

LAURA *(Slaps BONNIE across face):* Poor Hannah! That's all I've heard from you ever since she got here this afternoon! Is that *all* you can say?

   (Phone rings. BONNIE, on the verge of tears, starts for phone.) Don't answer it. It's that woman from the *Globe. (BONNIE starts to pick up the phone.)* DAMN IT, let it ring! *(LAURA intercepts BONNIE.)* I don't want anyone barging into this house and asking a lot of questions.

BONNIE: Everyone's going to know. Pretty soon you'll have to own up to Hannah!

LAURA: It's not Hannah I'm worried about. It's *me!*

BONNIE *(Beat):* You know, I'm just beginning to understand something about you . . . why you never got along with Daddy. Why you split up . . .

LAURA: So . . . that's what's bothering you.

BONNIE: When he came home and he wanted you back . . . and you wouldn't let him in the house? I just wanted to see you love each other. Was it so hard?

LAURA: Alright . . . I didn't love your father. Is that what you want me to say?

BONNIE: You weren't honest with him. How can you love if

you're not honest? I mean . . . you can't blot out a whole chunk of your life and expect to have a decent marriage!

LAURA: Aha! So now, suddenly, you are the expert on love and marriage!

BONNIE: You never even tried to make it work.

LAURA: What's gotten into you?

BONNIE: You just stood there and told me you never loved my father. *(Puts her hand to her cheek as if to ward off another blow.)* That's a terrible thing to say!

LAURA: You brought it up. *(Lights cigarette.)*

BONNIE: I never saw you hug him . . . or even touch. I used to think maybe you were just shy in front of me.

LAURA: You make me sound like some sort of freak.

BONNIE: There hasn't been another man, has there? Not since Daddy.

LAURA: You find that strange?

BONNIE: Yeah.

LAURA: I'm not capable of loving. Is that what you're trying to say? I'm cold and uncaring and unforgiving?

BONNIE: No, I'm just trying to understand you. I mean . . . when I told you I was staying with Nelson, you were ready to throw a fit.

LAURA: Alright . . . I admit I wasn't . . . overjoyed. You're still so young. And he's not my idea of a good, stable . . .

BONNIE: Welcome to the 80s, Mom. You've got some weird ideas.

LAURA: Maybe it's time you educate me.

BONNIE: Well, let's start right now. We plan to move in together. As soon as I finish school.

LAURA: Fine. If that's what you want. But remember, you can't come running home every time things go wrong.

BONNIE: You don't understand, Mother. Nelson loves me.

LAURA: That's just what I thought when I met your father. But once we signed the marriage license, all the sweetness . . . the gentility . . . the charm . . . just flew out the window.

BONNIE: Daddy was always gentle with me.

LAURA: Really? What about the weekend he dragged you down to Yarmouth. That broken-down shack he calls a beach house. With one of his . . . "teenyboppers." You didn't want to go, did you?

BONNIE: Please, Mother . . .

LAURA: Thank God I had the sense to drive down and haul you out of there.

BONNIE: You made a terrible scene. That "teenybopper" was a grown woman. And you accused him of statutory rape? I was humiliated!

LAURA: I wanted to protect you.

BONNIE: From what? From my father?

LAURA: You were just a child. When I was that age, I was thrown out on my own . . . with no one to look after me. I traveled all by myself. A child alone on a boat . . . going to a strange country. Boats can be dangerous . . . especially for children.

BONNIE: You're losing it!

LAURA: You think it's easy listening to all these accusations from my own daughter? I don't know how to love? I'm a liar and a freak?

BONNIE: I'm out of here. *(Goes to the closet, takes out coat and knapsack.)*

LAURA: What do you think you're doing? It's almost midnight.

BONNIE: You know where to find me.

LAURA: You're not doing anything of the sort.

BONNIE: Oh, yes I am. You thought you could lure me back to help you "cope" with everything. Well, you can damn well handle it by yourself.

LAURA: Your aunt was counting on you to take her sightseeing.

BONNIE: I feel sorry for you, Mother. You almost had me convinced. *(Putting on her coat)* I'll be back in the morning to pack.

LAURA: Why wait? *(Indicating stairs)* Be my guest!

BONNIE: I don't want to disturb Aunt Hannah! *(Slams the door as she exits.)*

The Moebius Band

JEAN STERRETT

A middle-aged woman has brought her old mother to a park on an outing from her Alzheimer's Care nursing home. Before the disease ameliorated the force of the mother's personality, the daughter had retreated into reserve as a defense against her mother's domination. Now, while the reserve persists, she is caught between conflicting feelings of compassion, irritation, and, possibly, love.

ISABEL: Thank you dear, this is lovely.
ANNE: Here's your napkin, Mum.
ISABEL: This is delicious, dear.
ANNE: Yes, it's very nice.
ISABEL: They must make a lot of money.
ANNE: Yes, I suppose they do.
    (A pause, while they eat.)
ISABEL: This is delicious, dear.
ANNE: Yes, it's very nice.
ISABEL: They must make a lot of money.
ANNE: Yes, I suppose they do.
ISABEL: Well, how's the world treating you, Anne dear?
ANNE: Fine.
ISABEL: I wish I could give you something.
ANNE: I don't need anything.
ISABEL: But I don't have any money.
ANNE: You have money, Mum.
ISABEL: Thank God!! Where did I get it?
ANNE: Social Security sends it.
ISABEL: No, I don't get anything.
ANNE: It's put in the bank on the first of each month.

ISABEL: But I haven't a penny in my purse.

ANNE: You don't need money in Waverley Hills. I pay for everything in advance.

ISABEL: But I have to have money in my pocket.

ANNE: Mum, it always gets lost in your room. Some of the ladies wander in and forget it belongs to you.

ISABEL: But I have to buy bread.

ANNE: You have all your meals in that nice dining room.

ISABEL: And milk.

ANNE: They do all the shopping.

ISABEL: But what if they ask me to pay?

ANNE: They won't ask you, Mum.

ISABEL: Are you sure?

ANNE: I'm sure.

ISABEL: But what if they ask me to pay?

ANNE: I've paid. I pay in advance.

ISABEL: Thank God! But I don't want to leave you short.

ANNE: I pay with your money, Mum.

ISABEL: I have no money, dear.

ANNE: Can't we talk about something else?

ISABEL: But I don't have a penny for food.

ANNE: Your meals are paid in advance.

ISABEL: Do they know?

ANNE: Yes they know.

ISABEL: Would you remind them, dear?

ANNE: I'd feel like a fool reminding them when they know I know they know.

ISABEL: Won't you just tell them you've paid for the dinner? In case they try to put one over?

ANNE: All right, all right, I'll tell them.

ISABEL: Thank God! You're a darling girl. I'm fond of all the family but, strangely enough, you're the one I love best.

ANNE: I don't think it's all that strange. I'm your only child.

ISABEL: You're a wonderful daughter.

ANNE: I know. A pearl beyond price!

(A beat, while ISABEL grasps the joke, titters.)

ISABEL: Yes dear, you're a . . . that thing . . . price.
(A beat. ISABEL points ahead.)
ISABEL: That's a pretty child.
ANNE: Uh huh.
ISABEL: She looks like the Princess Margaret Rose.
ANNE: She's a middle-aged woman, you know.
ISABEL: Oh yes, I clean forgot. . . . Any news from Mother?
(ANNE rises, stands for a minute, then walks downstage center as the light focuses in on her. She hesitates, kneels down, raises her hand to her forehead to make the sign of the cross, changes her mind, clasps her hands together. In dim light, ISABEL is seen eating ice cream throughout the following.)
ANNE: Bless me, Father, for I have sinned. . . . It's . . . uh . . . about thirty years since my last confession. Father, I want to confess a sin . . . a sin of the mind, it is. I've been wanting my mother's death. At first, the uh . . . thought would just flash past my mind, how it would feel to be free, but lately I've started to dwell on it. I don't love my mother. As a child, I worshipped her, but Father, I'm fifty-two years old and from all those years I can count on one hand the years that truly belonged to me. I don't feel guilt for not loving her. I feel the certainty of sin when I look at her eyes and imagine how cold and staring they'd be in death . . . and she smiles back at me and says, "Dear, you're so good . . . " (She stands up.) Father, I've taken too much of your time, coming in here on an impulse. If I'd stopped to think I'd have realized there's no earthly use your forgiving me if I can't forgive myself.
(Lights return to normal. ANNE is brought back to reality by ISABEL's repeated question.)
ISABEL: Any news from Mother?
ANNE: Your mother died, you know.
ISABEL: When?
ANNE: About twenty-five years ago, just after you left Australia.
ISABEL: Dear Mother, perhaps it's just as well. She doesn't have to worry. Have you heard from . . . you know, the other one?
ANNE: Your sister, Geraldine?

ISABEL: No, the one here in Sydney.

ANNE: This isn't Sydney; this is New York.

ISABEL: Oh yes, that's what I mean.

ANNE: I'm the only one that's here. The rest of the family's in Australia, except that Lucy's in London.

ISABEL: Who's Lucy, dear?

ANNE: Your granddaughter. Don't you remember? Remember Lucy's name for you?

ISABEL *(Delighted with the certainty of her name):* Isabel!

ANNE: She doesn't call you by your name; Lucy calls you Granbel. And what's your great granddaughter's name?

ISABEL: Mary?

ANNE: That was your mother's name.

ISABEL: Anne?

ANNE: I'm Anne.

ISABEL: I've just forgotten for the moment.

ANNE: Her name's Samantha. Sammy.

ISABEL: Dear, I'm worried. I haven't a penny.

ANNE: Let's talk about something else.

ISABEL: Just tell me how I get money.

ANNE: Mum, I've told you twenty times. You're making me want to scream.

ISABEL: Dear, don't scold me. Don't be angry. It spoils a pleasant outing.

ANNE: Now listen, Mum. I swear to you by all that's holy you have money in the bank and your bill at Waverley Hills is paid!

ISABEL: Thank God! Will you remind them, dear?

ANNE: All right, I'll remind them. We'll go back now and remind them.

> *(She helps ISABEL up and they start off.)*

ISABEL: It's been a lovely outing, dear. But this is the part I hate. Having to say goodbye to you.

ANNE: Well, I'll be back.

ISABEL: Will you come tomorrow?

ANNE: Mum, I can't come ev . . . Yes, I'll come tomorrow.

After the Wake

from *Alchemy of Desire/Dead-Man's Blues*

CARIDAD SVICH

Set in an open space reminiscent of a burnt-out bayou in the American South, Alchemy of Desire/Dead-Man's Blues *focuses on the emotional journey of a young woman named Simone, who must grapple with the wartime death of her husband, Jamie. In this scene, a community of women neighbors work and watch as Simone begins to struggle with Jamie's ghost. TIRASOL and CAROLINE are seated, shelling the last of a batch of beans into a large earthenware bowl. SELAH, a seer, and MIRANDA, a spirited woman in her late teens, are seated to one side. SELAH is fanning herself slowly. MIRANDA is looking out, listening. The bean shelling should serve as a kind of accompaniment to the voices—subtly, discreetly musical.*

TIRASOL: You know what they say?

CAROLINE: What they say?

TIRASOL: They say she made a pile of chicken bones in her backyard.

CAROLINE: That what they say?

TIRASOL: That's what they say.

> *(Beat)*

Know what else they say?

CAROLINE: What they say?

TIRASOL: They say she's goin round with no clothes on in the dead of night—

CAROLINE: No.

TIRASOL *(Continuing):* —callin his name out like he's gonna answer.

CAROLINE: They say that?

TIRASOL: I've heard it.

    (Beat)

CAROLINE: You lie.

TIRASOL: I swear on my mother's grave, may the poor woman rest in all-mighty peace.

CAROLINE: They say that?

TIRASOL: Uh-huh.

    (Beat)

CAROLINE: They sure say a lot of things.

SELAH: Don't mean it's true.

TIRASOL: Gotta mean somethin.

    (Beat)

SELAH: People talk.

TIRASOL: They talk all right.

SELAH: Talk until their tongues turn blue.

  Got NOTHIN

  to do.

    (Beans falling into bowl. Pause.)

TIRASOL: What's she gonna do?

MIRANDA: Who?

TIRASOL: Simone. What's she gonna do?

  GOT to do somethin. Ain't she?

  Can't keep grievin for-ever.

  Ain't do a soul no good to KEEP ON grievin.

  Bring nothin but chaos and misery on a person to do that.

  . . . What's she gonna do?

    (Beat)

CAROLINE: . . . Nothin.

TIRASOL: What you say?

CAROLINE: Nothin, I spect.

TIRASOL: Nothin?

CAROLINE: Uh-huh.

TIRASOL: What you mean, "nothin"?

  There ain't no such thing.

CAROLINE: Is, too.

TIRASOL: What? What you gonna tell me is "nothin"? Huh?

SELAH: . . . Goin on.

Lettin ourself just GO ON. That's a kind of nothin.

(To CAROLINE) Eh?

CAROLINE: Uh-huh.

(Beat)

TIRASOL: Bull. Throwing me bull, that's all you're doin.

That woman's GOT to do somethin.

. . .

Ain't even married a month.

SELAH: Mercy on the child.

CAROLINE: Have mercy.

MIRANDA: What's she gonna do?

(Pause)

TIRASOL: Heard say she wrote a letter to the guvment.

MIRANDA: Did what?

TIRASOL: Wrote a letter. Cussed them out.

MIRANDA: That true?

TIRASOL: It's true all right. I've heard it.

MIRANDA *(In thought):* . . . A letter . . .

TIRASOL: Yeh.

SELAH *(To herself):* Bull.

MIRANDA: What'd she say?

TIRASOL: Huh?

MIRANDA: What'd she say in this letter?

TIRASOL: She say all sorts of things.

Tell guvment this, that . . . Cussed them right out.

MIRANDA: Yeh?

TIRASOL: That's what they say.

MIRANDA *(In thought):* That's somethin.

TIRASOL: It's somethin all right.

MIRANDA: . . . Grand.

TIRASOL: Eh?

MIRANDA: Write somethin like that? To the guvment?

Grand, I say. Grand and valiant.

TIRASOL: Grand?

MIRANDA: Why, just the notion of it is . . . I couldn't do it.
   It may be a small measure of significance, but
   writin down a letter IS somethin.
SELAH: . . . Mercy on the child.
CAROLINE: Have mercy.
   (Pause)
TIRASOL: Got a right.
MIRANDA: Course she does.
CAROLINE: What you say?
TIRASOL: To cuss guvment out like that, it's a right.
CAROLINE: Got NO right.
TIRASOL: What you say now?
CAROLINE: Ain't guvment's fault. People die in wars all the time.
   She ain't the only one.
SELAH: That's right.
   (A second's pause)
CAROLINE: Your man, he passed on, didn't he?
SELAH: In the second war.
CAROLINE *(To herself)*: . . . the second war.
SELAH: Sweet boy, he was too. Never bring me no harm.
   Not like the other so-called men in my life.
   No, that boy was as good as can be.
   Hungry's all. Hungry for war.
   Couldn't wait to be part of it.
   Wanted the taste of battle more than anythin else,
   that boy. Wanted it more than lovin,
   more than any kind of lovin a woman could give him.
   I'd sit up at night and think, "That boy is a fool.
   What's he doin thinkin about war when he's got me
   ready to walk hot coals for him if I had to?
   What's he thinkin?. . ."
   But he didn't know no better.
   He was young. Young and hungry.
   A thirst for war is simply too much for a young man.
   It's a kind of call. A call to desperate livin.
   Boys listen to it. Their ears aflame:

O when the rapture of war come upon them unbelievable
in its truth.
Just didn't know no better.
. . . Sweet boy. Sweet sweet boy.
CAROLINE: . . . And he died.
SELAH: Yeh, he died. Fell out of a plane and into the sky,
body on fire. I don't think he ever saw the ground.
. . .
CAROLINE: And you ain't wrote the guvment.
SELAH: Nosir.
CAROLINE: It was your cross.
SELAH: Mine to bear.
CAROLINE: You just moved on.
SELAH: Had to. Couldn't write.
Couldn't write. Couldn't read. Not at the time.
CAROLINE: You just moved on.
SELAH: Ye-ah.
(Pause)
MIRANDA: Ain't easy.
SELAH: Movin on? Not a thing easy about it.
Gotta walk all over your past to move on.
TIRASOL: Gotta do it, though.
SELAH: f you wanna live in the present, yeh.
Some folks never get out of their past:
they just stay there in permanent memory:
waitin their time until they die.
s not livin. Livin's hard.
Hard and mean and full of rapturous pleasure.
MIRANDA: Can get crazy, though.
SELAH: Yeh. Can make you wander—
wander so far you forget where you're goin.
MIRANDA: What you do, then?
SELAH: Get your past and present to come together, I spect.
Course, there's all different kinds of wanderin.
Some wanderin . . . : Well, let's just say,
it ain't a matter of forgettin,

so much as, a matter of rememberin
where you stopped in the first place.
TIRASOL *(To herself):* Amen to that.
  (Beat)
CAROLINE: Child could go crazy, if all this talk is true.
  Could go mad.
TIRASOL: Oh, it's true. I've heard it, it's true.
SELAH: She keep thinkin about him, yeh. She don't . . .
  (Pause)
TIRASOL: He was a stupid boy.
MIRANDA: Was not.
TIRASOL: Stupid. Didn't know anythin, that boy:
  always walkin around, not a thought in his brain.
SELAH: She loved him.
CAROLINE: Yeh, she did.
SELAH: He loved her.
MIRANDA: . . . Don't know bout that.
CAROLINE: You say he didn't?
TIRASOL: I say he was stupid. Don't think he knew what love was,
  cept for puttin his thing between a woman's legs.
MIRANDA *(In thought):* . . . He could do that.
  (Beat)
CAROLINE: Oh, child.
  You just run wild. Got no mind at all.
MIRANDA: Ain't married him. Got some mind to do that.
TIRASOL *(To herself):* Sleepin with the devil.
  Sleepin in the devil's bed.
SELAH: Mercy.
CAROLINE: Mercy on the child.
MIRANDA: It's war.
  Wartime makes you wild.
  (Pause)
TIRASOL: Say, you know where was that war?
MIRANDA: Which war?
TIRASOL: This war.
MIRANDA: Don't know. Some country, I spect.

TIRASOL: . . . China?

MIRANDA: No. China's at the bottom of the ground,
    clear way to the other side of the earth,
    you gotta dig to find it. Not China.

CAROLINE: I used to know where it was.

TIRASOL: Yeh?

CAROLINE: Used to know xactly where it was.
    Can't remember the name.
    How come names do that?

MIRANDA: Do what?

CAROLINE: Escape us?

TIRASOL: Too many countries.

SELAH: Too many wars.
        (Pause)

TIRASOL: What's she doin now, I wonder?
    Got no talk to tell me.

CAROLINE: Don't know. Don't know nothin no more.
    . . .

SELAH: I spect she's sleepin. Gotta sleep off your mournin.
    Only way to stop the ghosts from hauntin you.

TIRASOL: Sleepin. Yeh. Could be doin that.

MIRANDA: I spect she's dreamin.

TIRASOL: Dreamin?
    What she gonna be dreamin about with her grievin?
    She got no cause to dream.

MIRANDA: She got cause.

TIRASOL: Yeh?

MIRANDA: She's dreamin.

TIRASOL: What's she dreamin about?

MIRANDA: She's dreamin of his sweet eyes lookin at her . . .
    his tongue, his mouth . . .
    dreamin.

CAROLINE: You need some water, child. Gotta cool yourself off.

MIRANDA: It's hot.

CAROLINE: No excuse for talk like that.
    That's a dead-man you're talkin about.

Gotta respect the dead same as the livin.

MIRANDA: Ain't said nothin.

CAROLINE: Said plenty, that mouth of yours.
You got no right to talk bout that man,
especially not about his body.
The man is dead. His body is in the ground.
Ain't no dreamin of any kind about a dead-man's body.
Especially not when he's left a widow to remember him by.

MIRANDA: You sayin she ain't dreamin?

CAROLINE: I'm sayin: you gotta conduct yourself,
no matter how much you ache for him.
   (Pause)

TIRASOL: Hot.

CAROLINE: Yeh.

MIRANDA *(To herself):* And she's dreamin. . . .

CAROLINE: Mercy.

SELAH: Mercy on the child.

A Smoke and a Line

from *Alchemy of Desire/Dead-Man's Blues*

CARIDAD SVICH

SIMONE, a young woman who has been recently widowed, is seated by the water, fishing. MIRANDA, a spirited woman in her late teens who once had a brief fling with SIMONE's late husband, walks in. She has been sent by Selah, the town seer, to check on SIMONE's state of mind.

MIRANDA: Ain't caught anythin yet?

SIMONE: Not yet.

MIRANDA: Gotta be patient. Gotta wait.

SIMONE: Mmm-hmm.

MIRANDA: I used to go fishin, so I know.

SIMONE: Yeh?

    (MIRANDA nods. Beat.)

MIRANDA: Never actually fished myself, mind you.

SIMONE: Huh?

MIRANDA: My grammy'd take me. When I was little.
  She's the one did the actual fishin.
  I'd just watch her. *(Pulls out a cigarette)* Smoke?

SIMONE: No.

MIRANDA: Yeh, she'd take me. I didn't know what was goin on.
  I used to say, "Grammy, what's this? Grammy, what's that?"
  "Hush, child," she'd say, "hush."
    (MIRANDA lights a cigarette, smokes.)

SIMONE *(To herself):* Hush. . . .

MIRANDA: Swear don't know how she put up with me, but she did.
  She'd just smile . . . sit there . . . fish.
  She'd smoke, too.

Not cigarettes, but a big ol cigar bout this thick.
You should've seen the smoke she'd blow out of that thing.
Swirls and swirls of it. Like chimney smoke.
And it smelled, too.
Not sweet like Caroline's perfume, but strong.
Like dust and ginger.
SIMONE: Yeh?
MIRANDA: Used to make 'em herself, the cigars.
Grow the tobacco out back,
roll the leaves up in the finest paper—
suck on it 'til one end'd be completely wet
with her saliva and juice, and then she'd light up,
the raw tobacco just envelopin the air.
Oh, and she'd smile . . . she'd smile the biggest grin . . .
Teeth turned black, she'd still smile.
I hated it. All of it. The cigars. Everythin.
Felt like it was a punishment every time I had to go out
with her. Grammy and her goddam tobacco.
But after a while, I don't know how it occurred,
the smell of that tobacco became like heaven itself.
"When we goin fishin, Grammy? When we goin?"
"Patience, child. Patience." And she'd smile,
gather her gear, and take me down to the water.
The sun'd be comin up. You could see the rays just peerin.
Flashes of light bouncin off the water blindin you as you
looked into the mornin haze. And she'd smile,
lay out the tobacco, and start rollin them cigars,
her hands movin sharp and quick like one of those
gunfighters on the TV all eyes and trigger fingers.
Rollin and lightin up. Smokin and castin a line.
It was all of a piece with Grammy.
I'd sit there, wallowin in the smell,
swear all angels had come down to pay us a visit.
Used to try to catch the rings of smoke with my mouth,
like some sort of weird human kind of fish.
I must've caught a hundred rings one time. One hundred.

I swear, it was the best part of goin fishin.
n fact, for the longest time,
that's what I thought fishin was:
just somethin you did to go smokin.
   (Beat)
SIMONE: Wouldn't she catch anythin?
MIRANDA: Every once in a while, sure.
   Caught a yellow perch once—
   gutted it, chopped it up, ate it for supper.
   But I can't say I remember her actually catchin
   much of anythin in particular.
   Not like you see in those pictures they got
   all over the walls at the diner
   of people standin tall next to their big fish
   and smilin.
   Can't say she ever got took a picture like that.
SIMONE: It's the water.
MIRANDA: Yeh.
SIMONE: Ain't made for monster fish.
MIRANDA: That it ain't.
   Not like in other parts.
   In other parts, you got water so wide
   there's almost too much room for big fish to swim round.
SIMONE: . . . I'd like to see that.
MIRANDA: What?
SIMONE: Wide water. No fence.
   You fish in that, gotta come up with somethin.
MIRANDA: You been in other parts, though.
SIMONE: Yeh, but not with that kind of water.
   Most parts I been . . . just land:
   flat, rough land. No sign of water.
MIRANDA: Well, she says it's wide. Kind of water you can get lost
   in, if you're not careful.
SIMONE: Wouldn't mind that.
MIRANDA: What?
SIMONE: Gettin lost.

MIRANDA: I'd mind.

SIMONE: Yeh?

MIRANDA: Think I'd be scared not knowin where I was.
Don't think I'd like too much bein at the mercy of
water.

SIMONE: Better than not being anythin.

(Beat)

MIRANDA: . . . Got somethin?

SIMONE: Feels like somethin's on the line.

MIRANDA: Maybe you got somethin.

SIMONE: . . . It's gone.

MIRANDA: That happens. Used to happen to Grammy all the time.
Just when she'd think a fish bite, it'd go away.
They're not as stupid as we think—fish.
I mean, if I were a fish,
I wouldn't want to be somebody's supper.
I'd know better than to jump at the first thing I saw.
. . .
What you thinkin?

SIMONE: Hmm?

MIRANDA: What you thinkin?

SIMONE: . . . Nothin.

MIRANDA: Awful quiet. Gotta be thinkin bout somethin.

SIMONE: Just thinkin.

MIRANDA: What about?

SIMONE: . . . Thinkin bout the world.

MIRANDA: The world? What you thinkin bout the world?

SIMONE: . . . Thinkin that it's some place, y'know.
That it's such a big place, and all these things happen—
wars, fires, hurricanes, sickness—
I think, "How come the soil don't just BURST?
How come it don't just burst from all this excitement?"
I know I would.
If it were me, I'd EXPLODE in a thousand little pieces,
scatter myself in bits all over the earth—
wars, fires, hurricanes comin up out of me

in BILE colored gray, scarlet, and indigo.
Come up and out of me
til there'd be NOTHIN, just open space:
a whole other world.
I don't know how the soil can take it. I really don't.
    (Beat)
MIRANDA: Selah says the soil's stronger than all of us,
    on account of that's where we go once we pass on.
    . . . And that's where we get our strength, too,
    from the soil.
SIMONE: Yeh?
MIRANDA: That's what she says.
SIMONE: . . . How you get strength from somethin that's torn
    apart,
    BUSTED open? How you get it then?
MIRANDA: . . . Maybe a different soil come up.
SIMONE: Huh?
MIRANDA: A different soil, a different earth underneath the old
    one. Maybe it'd come up and . . . I don't know, it'd do
    somethin.
    (Beat. They listen for a moment.)
    What you think?
SIMONE: Hmm?
MIRANDA *(Identifying sound in the distance):* What you think?
    Car?
SIMONE *(Listens, then:):* Motor-cycle.
MIRANDA: Yeh?
SIMONE: Engine. Sounds different.
MIRANDA: Better, huh?
    (SIMONE nods.)
    Wonder where it was headin.
SIMONE *(To herself):* Wide water.
    . . .
    Damn.
MIRANDA: Fish ain't jumpin for nothin, huh?
    They'll come round.

Grammy'd sometimes have to wait two, three hours
before a fish jump.

That's when she'd really put her time in smokin.

(Offering another cigarette) You sure you don't want one?

   (SIMONE shakes her head.)

It's good.

SIMONE: I know.

   (Beat)

MIRANDA: So, what you do, you clean the house yet?

SIMONE: . . . No.

MIRANDA: Gotta clean it.

SIMONE: Ain't gotta DO nothin.

MIRANDA: Selah says you don't clean a house after someone's—

SIMONE: Hell what Selah says! I ain't doin it. Ain't goin in there.

MIRANDA: Well, she says if you don't clean it, you collect bad
   spirits.

And then you can't even go into the house.

Even if you want to.

Gotta BURN IT DOWN. Cause fire's the only thing
that'll scare bad spirits off for good.

SIMONE: She say that?

MIRANDA: Yeh. And she said you don't get rid of bad spirits,
   they come round and turn on you—turn you into a SPOOK.

SIMONE: I ain't a spook.

MIRANDA: That's what she said.

SIMONE: Well, I ain't!

Hell, who wants to be that?

Nobody talkin to you, nobody lookin at you—
nobody wants that.

   (Beat)

MIRANDA: So, you gonna clean it?

Hmm?

   . . .

SIMONE *(Referring to fish):* I think I got somethin.

MIRANDA: Yeh?

SIMONE: Yeh.

MIRANDA: See? The livin are comin back to you.

SIMONE: Huh?

MIRANDA: The livin. They're comin' back.

Winnie and G

ANASTASIA TRAINA

WINNIE and GEANNIE are estranged cousins from working class families. WINNIE is single and self-educated, with an air of good breeding and the spirit of an explorer. GEANNIE is a mother of two, a simple and honest woman who yearns for more. The two women are sitting in a doctor's waiting room. GEANNIE has come to discuss the results of her mammography. WINNIE surprises her by showing up to give her support. The two have not seen each other in ten years.

GEANNIE: You know Win, when I was lying there a moment ago things were flooding through my brain like a fuckin lightning storm. Like when we were kids in Long Beach and we used to lock ourselves in the bathroom, remember? We would smoke like bandits lit on fire . . .

WINNIE: I remember alright. It's all your fault if I'm a cigarette addict. You're the one who told me that I didn't inhale. Remember?

GEANNIE: Don't blame your dependency on me. And when you did, you got so dizzy that you fell right into the bathtub. I also remember how you used to stuff your bra because you were flatter than my mother's potato pancakes. Then you used to tug on those little titties so hard because you wanted them to hang like grandma's. You thought her sagging breasts were soooooooooooo beautiful . . . Ahh . . . We wanted to grow up so fast. We couldn't wait.

WINNIE: Yeah.

GEANNIE: Now what I wouldn't give . . .

WINNIE: Yeah . . . *(Pause)* Did it hurt, that mammo thing?

GEANNIE: Nah, compared to breast feeding it's a breeze. I can't get over the fact that you came. How did you know where I was?

WINNIE: You told me the address . . . .

GEANNIE: Yeah, but I don't remember telling you the name.

WINNIE: You didn't. But I thought to myself what the hell. At least I can say I tried with a clear conscience. But I didn't know there were so many doctors in this building. So, I asked the elevator man if he knew what floor the doctor who takes care of *(Miming breast)* was on. And he said, "Oh yeah, eleventh floor, Dr. Sarry." What a name huh?

GEANNIE: Yeah huh? Marie told me this guy is the best. I think she was right. I like his bedside manner. Smooth as a duck's egg. Am I right or wrong? That's what's wrong with these young doctors today, they have no manners. Plus this guy is an artist. Did you see that piece of sculpture out in the hall there?

WINNIE: This?

GEANNIE: Yeah. He did that.

WINNIE: What's she doing holding on to her breast like that for?

GEANNIE: She's giving herself an examination.

WINNIE: That's wonderful. Where did Marie get his name from?

GEANNIE: You know Marie's mother died of breast cancer?

WINNIE: No, I didn't know . . .

GEANNIE: Yeah . . . Anyway this is the same guy that took care of Marie's mother.

WINNIE: I see . . . she died?

GEANNIE: Oh yeah, she was in her nineties God bless her soul.

WINNIE: You want some coffee?

GEANNIE: No thanks . . . Is it decaf? No, forget it, they probably only have Cremora. You go ahead and have some.

WINNIE: I really shouldn't. I had three cups already. My heart is buzzing faster than a speeding bee.

GEANNIE: I go to church every Sunday, I buy everything organic, I don't drink or smoke . . . This is the work of the devil. He always has to screw things up just when things are going your way. . . . What did I do to deserve this? Oh, God! I feel my throat closin up on me, I can't breathe.

WINNIE: It's just anxieties.

GEANNIE: You think?

WINNIE: Yeah. Here repeat after me. Do what I do. I AM THE LIGHT. THE LIGHT IS ALL AROUND ME. Just try it. What do you have to lose? I AM THE LIGHT. THE LIGHT IS ALL AROUND ME. THE LIGHT IS MY PROTECTOR. I FEEL THE LIGHT. I WALK WITH THE LIGHT . . . . Now don't forget to breathe. That's it. In . . . Out. Breathe . . . .

GEANNIE: Wow, that's powerful stuff. I gotta remember that one. You better stop smokin!

WINNIE: If one more person tells me I should stop smoking, I'm gonna ram their fuckin brains in! Don't you think I know it's bad for me! I know! . . . I only smoke three or four a day now.

GEANNIE: I was only thinking about your health . . . .

WINNIE: I know. I'm just touchy about it, that's all.

GEANNIE: Yeah, I never seen you lose your composure like that. What's the matter?

WINNIE: Nothing.

GEANNIE: Don't tell me nothing. Don't forget I grew up with you. I know you better than my own self.

WINNIE: I've been trying to have a baby, that's all.

GEANNIE: You! Want a baby?

WINNIE: What's so funny about that?

GEANNIE: Nothing, nothing at all. It just never occurred to me. . . . I mean your life is so full and everything . . . not to mention the obvious.

WINNIE: Yoko Ono did it when she was fifty. . . .

GEANNIE: Yeah, but did she smoke for twentysome-odd years?

WINNIE: With modern science anything is possible if you have enough cash. And I do. Why don't we just leave it at that.

GEANNIE: Yeah, but you, a mother . . . Why would you want to muck up a perfectly good . . . life?

WINNIE: Being a mother is one of the most beautiful things a woman can do. It's like . . . it's like the ultimate garden. It's like watching a delicate orchid blossoming. And when they call out, "Mommy." Intoxicating, that's what it is . . . .

GEANNIE: Yeah, it's easy for you; easy for you to say. But the bottom line is people don't have any respect for mothers nowadays. Believe me when I tell you it ain't poetry when you have to change their shitty diapers and your husband never lifts a finger to help. If I could just erase time, I'd do my life over differently. I'd travel like you did. I'd be somebody like you.

WINNIE: What are you talking about? You are somebody.

GEANNIE: No, I'm not. I don't have any idea of who I really am. I never had the chance to find out. I never followed my dreams. I wanted to sing. . . .

WINNIE: You can still do that . . . dreams don't die. . . .

GEANNIE: No, they just become faded shadows so far off in the distance . . . ah what's the use! *(Pause)* Why didn't you take me with you when you went away?

WINNIE: Why bring that up? It was so long ago. . . . To be quite honest, it wasn't all that peachy and creamy.

GEANNIE: Yeah but to travel the world like you did. Just fuck everything and everyone . . . Ya gotta be selfish in this world. . . . Ya gotta be a fuckin bitch if you want ta get . . .

WINNIE: My Lord, the time is just crawling like a snail on its last leg. This is the part that I really hate.

GEANNIE: Really, you feel like it's going slow? I think it's going pretty quickly. Winnie, so long as we're here why don't you get a checkup?

WINNIE: I don't think so.

(Silence.)

GEANNIE: Do you remember that doll that came out in the 50s, she was called Little Miss No Name?

WINNIE: No.

GEANNIE: Oh come on, sure you do. She wore an apron and she had a tear rollin down her cheek.

WINNIE: No, can't say I remember her.

GEANNIE: She was the only doll I ever had. I saw her the other day in this antiques shop on Henry Street. Do you know how much they wanted for that doll? Two hundred and fifty dollars. I was goin to buy her, but who has that kinda money to spend on a doll? I wonder why my mother never saved her.

WINNIE: Have you ever thought of seeing somebody?

GEANNIE: You mean like a therapist? I don't need a therapist. They're only for crazy people. I'm not crazy. (Pause) Oh my God, what is that? It's a centipede!

WINNIE: That's not a centipede. That's an earwig.

GEANNIE: They're dangerous! They crawl up inside your brain and make you lose your mind!

WINNIE: Who told you that?

GEANNIE: It's true. In the movie of *The Hunchback of Notre Dame* that's what drove the hunchback crazy, earwigs.

WINNIE: Well, you can relax now it's gone.

GEANNIE: Yeah, but where did it go? (Pause) I don't know why you even bothered comin . . .

WINNIE: You wanna know why I came.

GEANNIE: Yeah, I would really like to know! Lower your voice—people can hear you.

WINNIE: You wanna know. I'll tell you why I came. Because, because time and time again I keep hoping, praying I'll fit in. . . . I'm just like some moronic woman who buys a size ten shoe when she's really a size eleven. I'm banging my head against a cement wall . . . looking for some hint, some semblance of a family. A family feeling, anything. But I'm just fucking fooling myself. I'm just a big stupid fool.

GEANNIE: Don't give me that pure of heart Tiny Tim bullshit. Why didn't you think about family when you were trotting all over the world? When you left I cried and cried and cried . . .

WINNIE: Did you cry because you missed me or because it wasn't you?

GEANNIE: Tou-fuckin-ché! Fuck. Fuck me! I fucked up. I have a fucked-up mind. I'm fucked. I'm a selfish fuckin bitch. I'm really fucked. Fuck it.

WINNIE: You're trying to express something to me.

GEANNIE: Let's change the subject. I have a fucking splitting headache. My head fucked . . . is fuckin split right here, right down the middle.

WINNIE: I'm not afraid, OK?

GEANNIE: OK.

WINNIE: I'm not.

GEANNIE: Got it. *(Pause)* Is your new boyfriend going on this tour with you?

WINNIE: Yeah, he's coming.

GEANNIE: I wish my husband was more like that. He's always tired when he comes home from work. All he does is sit in front of the TV with the sports channel blasting at full speed. I don't know . . . .

WINNIE: Your husband is a very nice guy . . .

GEANNIE: Oh, don't get me wrong, I love my husband. He's a nice guy and all. He really is a nice guy. He's so nice he sent the Knicks a Mass card from St. Jude wishing them luck in the playoffs.

WINNIE: I heard about that.

GEANNIE: So you also heard about him searching out the grave of Judy Garland so that he could sing to her "Over the Rainbow."

WINNIE: No, I didn't hear that. That's good, he's gettin in touch with his feminine side.

GEANNIE: Yeah . . .

WINNIE: It's lucky we don't pay these doctors by the hour, we'd really be in some deep financial shit.

GEANNIE: The best of the best was when he put the urn of our cat Fini in front of the TV for the Stanley Cup. He was screaming, "Go Rangers! Go! I got my Fini up in heaven looking after yas! It's a no-lose situation." I'll tell ya. It's a wonder I haven't left the screwball sooner. I think I married below my standin.

WINNIE: You want to leave your husband?

GEANNIE: Truthfully Win . . . What am I doing? I'm wasting my life. I'm telling you, you're my witness if everything turns out OK with these here tests. I'm turning over a new tea leaf. I'm gonna pack my bags and take my two kids and we're getting out. We're going far far away.

WINNIE: You don't mean that.

GEANNIE: Oh no? Watch me. I'm gonna live live live live. If there is one thing this thing has taught me it's time is all we got, and not a lot of it either. Who knows when our sand's gonna run out.

WINNIE: Don't be nonsensical. Where are you going with two kids strapped to your shoelaces?

GEANNIE: Other women do it all the time. I'll find a job . . .

WINNIE: Doing what?

GEANNIE: I was a very good dental hygienist, for your information.

WINNIE: I know.

GEANNIE: I was.

(Silence. GEANNIE starts to cry. WINNIE takes out a cigarette.)
Don't you light that cigarette in here!

WINNIE: I'm not.

GEANNIE: I can't believe you came.

WINNIE: I said I'd be here.

GEANNIE: Win, did you ever think about milk when it turns sour?

WINNIE: What?

GEANNIE: You know curdled milk? Like when is that moment, when the milk is good, that those little molecules choose to change?

WINNIE: I honestly can't answer . . . that. G, you want to know the truth. I am afraid. I'm afraid every waking day.

NURSE'S VOICE *(Off):* The doctor is ready for you. If you'll please follow me.

(GEANNIE turns to WINNIE.)

WINNIE: It's about time.

(GEANNIE starts to leave and abruptly turns back to WINNIE.)

GEANNIE: Before I go in I wanna ask you something very personal. I know you never talk about it . . . to anyone and no one ever asks you . . .

WINNIE: Yeah.

GEANNIE: Your father . . . he's been gone a long time now . . . and you were just a baby when he died. . . . Do you . . . I mean . . . ever think about him?

WINNIE: There won't be a day that goes by that your kids won't think about you.

GEANNIE: Thanks.

(GEANNIE starts to exit. WINNIE watches her go.)

WINNIE: Piece of cake.

Organic Form

from *Ikebana*

ALICE TUAN

ROSE, 81, is putting together a puzzle of Walden Pond. She uses a magnifying glass to examine each piece. She is searching for border pieces. Her daughter ESTER sits separately, moisturizing her arms and legs.

ROSE: AH! Corner.
>*(10 count pause)*

Good! Another corner.

ESTER: The feng shui master . . .

ROSE: Two more.

ESTER: Master Li. I called Master Li. . . .

ROSE: Straight, good! More, more . . .

ESTER: He is your friend, Mr. Li, isn't he? Ma, Mr. Li?

ROSE: What?

ESTER: Feng shui Master Li?

ROSE: Your son gives me this, what is it? 500 pieces. Everything blue, blue. What is this Wal-Den-Pon lake? The sky is blue, the lake is blue, only a little little red and gold for trees but everything, everything else . . . blue!

ESTER: Then don't do it.

ROSE: He said, 'together, Grandma, together.' Where *is* he?

ESTER: He's busy.

ROSE: Line busy, busy. Everybody all grown up. They drive. They drive their cars. Never visit Grandma . . .

ESTER: He's fixing my door.

ROSE: It's broken?

ESTER: Master Li says my door is in a bad . . . position. We need to rearrange the angle, three inches south.

ROSE: All the bad things have already happened. Dexter dead. Luther dead. Your baby dead. Daddy dead. Me, no descendants. What more?

ESTER: I want to prevent further . . .

ROSE: Is this sky blue or lake blue? I can't tell.

(ROSE throws the piece over her shoulder. ESTER picks it up and returns it to the table.)

ESTER: I think Master Li should come here and see that your house is in a healthier arrangement.

ROSE: Don't put that in the lake pile!

ESTER: For your health, Ma.

(ROSE pounds a piece in.)

That doesn't fit.

ROSE: It does now. I can make a picture with just 300 pieces.

ESTER: Rock will be upset.

ROSE: Who?

ESTER: Your grandson.

ROSE: You call him what? A Rock?

ESTER: I heard his friend at the door call him that.

ROSE *(Attentive):* A girlfriend?

ESTER: Sounded like . . .

ROSE: Maybe a wife.

ESTER: He's just a baby.

ROSE: He's ready to breed.

ESTER: Ma!

ROSE: Young people, really young . . . teenagers. Getting pregnant. Everybody else's line drawn, but mine has stopped at a dot. That Violet should just marry that Ph.D. boy.

ESTER: She wants to sing.

ROSE: She can sing to her babies.

ESTER: The Ph.D. boy has gone away.

ROSE: She should follow him. Where did he go?

ESTER: Brown University.

ROSE: Ivy League Ph.D.

ESTER *(Whispers):* He's Japanese.

ROSE: In America, it still looks Chinese. How about this girl who calls your son Rock. Is she Chinese?

ESTER: I was sleeping.

ROSE: You heard her say Rock?

ESTER: Yes . . . he was, she was . . . now that I . . . maybe I heard it in my dream.

ROSE: You sleep too much.

(Pound pound pound the puzzle pieces in. LILY, ROSE's elder daughter, enters with groceries.)

LILY: Ma. Ester.

ESTER: Let me help you Lily.

LILY: It's too heavy for you. What's Ma pounding on now?

ESTER: We haven't seen you for weeks, Lily.

LILY: You just stay.

ROSE *(Stops pounding):* Oh Lily. You're here.

LILY: This is bad for your eyes.

ESTER: Where have you been Lily?

LILY: What lake is this?

ESTER: We called and called . . .

LILY: Is Woodman here?

ROSE: He's courting that woman I hate.

LILY: Beatrice did nothing to you.

ESTER: Busy at work, Lily?

LILY: I've been busy at church.

ROSE: He's not coming back.

LILY: I have prayers that he will. Luther is only missing. He's not dead. Ester, you want to help put groceries away?

ROSE: What horrible thing are you going to tell Ester about me, Lily?

LILY: No, no. It's just . . . we haven't seen each other in a while . . .

ROSE: You hate each other. You never talk—beyond the petty.

LILY: Just want to catch her up about some things, Ma. That's all.

ROSE: It always worries me, Lily, when you speak so nicely to me. What do you want to tell Ester that you can't tell me?

LILY: Nothing, nothing . . . church things. You don't like to hear about church things I know. God is a crock, you say, and I respect that but . . .

ROSE: Don't try to drag Ester into your church world. She doesn't believe in that stuff, do you Ester? Do you . . .

ESTER: You're right, Mother. Ever since Dexter . . . and then Lucy . . . you're right. There is no God, there is none when half of my family can be taken away, just like that.

LILY: Called to duty . . .

ROSE: Oh bullshit.

LILY: Ma! Ester is a grown woman. Why do you demand she always agree with you? All this . . . this . . . suppression is probably what gave her *(Stop)*
(ROSE puts the magnifying glass down, turns and looks at LILY.)

ROSE: Gave her what, Lily?
(10 count pause)
Gave her what? Do you have something Ester?

ESTER: Yeah. *(Beat)* Bad luck.

ROSE: So I'm the one who gave her bad luck?

LILY: I bought your week's food for you. Fish, chicken, nothing salty . . .

ROSE: So what? You don't have to. I didn't ask you.

LILY: Fine. Here. Take it.

ROSE: What's happened to your Christian spirit, Lily? To give with a smile and ask nothing in return.

ESTER: Come Lily. I'll help you put groceries away.

ROSE: Grown woman, Lily. All these baby tears.

ESTER: No, stay, stay Lily. We'll put the puzzle together.

LILY: Yes, God gives me strength to continue.
(ESTER and LILY exit to offstage kitchen.)

ROSE: god god god. What is this god. Here, god, this is the pile with the sky. Where you arrange the helpless, like my daughter the Christian. Good plan. Make them depend on you.

Put the fear in them and they won't say a bad thing against you. I understand you god. That's why you're not needed. HEAVEN! . . . has yet to be put together.

(She scoots the sky pieces off the table.)

There god, there you are. God is everywhere! *(Laughs)*

Southern Belle

ALANA VALENTINE

CARSON MCCULLERS has traveled to New York from her home town of Columbus, Georgia, in search of adventure and fame as a writer. Her muse, Frankie, who appears as a character in the play, has urged CARSON to go along to The North Star, a night-club. The scene is the interior of the club. CARSON is sitting at a table reading a book. VERONICA VANDROSS enters and goes over to CARSON.

VERONICA: You're new around here, aren't you?

CARSON: Yes, I am.

VERONICA: Do you mind if I sit down?

CARSON: No.

(Veronica sits.)

VERONICA: Are you from around here?

CARSON: Yes. I'm living here at the moment.

VERONICA: But you're from the South, aren't you?

CARSON: Yes. I am.

VERONICA: You must find it very different.

CARSON: Like night and day.

VERONICA: Yes and in that order. What brings you here?

CARSON: I'm learning to be a writer.

VERONICA: A writer. So explain the world to me. So how is it different here from life on the farm?

CARSON: The difference has to do with certain freedoms. The freedom to plant whatever you like in your own vegetable patch.

VERONICA: And if you want to plant flowers you can do that too.

CARSON: Of course. In Georgia anyone with any sense plants tomatoes.

VERONICA: How precisely you articulate it. You are clever at describing things.

CARSON: Yes. I am.

VERONICA: That impresses me a great deal.

CARSON: Thank you.

VERONICA: It excites you doesn't it? *(Carson nods.)* Being here.

CARSON: It's intoxicating.

VERONICA: Being here with me.

CARSON: Yes.

VERONICA: Do you know what I am?

CARSON: I think so.

VERONICA: And you are attracted to me.

CARSON: Yes. Very much.

VERONICA: What's your sexual preference?

CARSON: It never occurred to me to cultivate one.

VERONICA: How old are you?

CARSON: Eighteen.

VERONICA: Well, you should have some idea.

CARSON: I do. Well, I have a theory. You see I don't necessarily fall in love with men or women. I fall in love with the spirit of a thing.

VERONICA: I see. Well that counts me out honey. I'm afraid I draw the line at inanimate objects.

CARSON: I'm not talking about inanimate objects.

VERONICA: What's your name?

CARSON: Carson. I think there are some people, and I am one of them, who fall in love with a person for where they are in their life and your life and the world.

VERONICA: Well of course, Carson, that's why you don't fall in love with everyone you meet. But you do have preferences, don't you?

CARSON: I think it's all a matter of the individual.

VERONICA: I think that's all very well when you're talking about love or obsession but I, my darling Carson, was talking about sex and when it comes to sex I think people have definite preferences about what gives them pleasure in the sack.

CARSON: So wonderfully direct.

VERONICA: Excuse me?

CARSON: Your replies, they're so direct. In Columbus I wouldn't even be able to talk about this sort of stuff without being . . .

VERONICA: Lynched?

CARSON: Just about.

VERONICA: Yes, the South, where people are about as enthusiastic about intelligent debate as I am about constipation. The glorious South where discussions about sexuality are about as rare as black millionaires.

CARSON: The South is beginning to change, you know.

VERONICA: The place is a cesspool of bigotry. Small-minded power brokers greasing their own palms and fussing over their families.

CARSON: And the North is so different?

VERONICA: No place is any different. Don't tell me you're going to try to defend the place?

CARSON: Southerners can be very loyal.

VERONICA: When have they ever been loyal to you?

CARSON: And people are a lot friendlier.

VERONICA: When you agree not to speak your mind.

CARSON: Just stop attacking the South.

VERONICA: Why should I?

CARSON: Because it's still my home!

　　(Pause)

VERONICA: Look, I'm sorry. I thought you were living here at the moment.

CARSON: I am.

VERONICA: Sure. Look, let me make it up to you over a glass of gin. You like gin?

CARSON: Sure.

VERONICA: I've got a bottle at my place, it's just around the block.

CARSON: Why don't you just buy me one here?

VERONICA: I can't afford the prices. Look, if I've offended you, I'll just leave you alone.

CARSON: No . . . well . . . OK . . .

VERONICA: I'll just get my coat.

> *(Lights down on the club and up on a bed. CARSON and VERONICA walk over to the bed. CARSON sits on the end of it while VERONICA lies in the middle. They both have glasses of gin.)*

CARSON: So, what's your name?

VERONICA: Veronica, Veronica Vandross.

CARSON: This is good gin.

VERONICA: Would you like some more?

CARSON: No.

VERONICA: Tell me, Carson, do you have any idea about your sexual preferences yet?

CARSON: Not really.

VERONICA: How about this individual then?

CARSON: Not really. Is that terrible for you?

VERONICA: Not at all.

CARSON: I must seem like such a hick.

VERONICA: That's not true. Plenty of women get to the end of the bed and still don't know whether they want to keep going.

CARSON: Are you sure?

VERONICA: Sure. And it's always my bed that they seem to hesitate at.

CARSON: Really?

VERONICA: Just a little joke. *(Pause)* A friend of mine told me that a woman almost went to bed with her the other night but stopped herself because she thought she might never want to go to bed with men again if she did.

CARSON: Well that's right.

VERONICA: But isn't that something you might want to know?

CARSON: Yes, of course, then again you might want to keep going to bed with both sexes.

VERONICA: That's always a risk.

CARSON: I don't think I can, Veronica, at least not tonight.

> *(Short pause)*

VERONICA: More gin? Yes, don't mind if I do.

CARSON: Are you very angry?

VERONICA: Shall we be passionately good friends and ring each other and write to each other and rave endlessly to our friends about each other?

CARSON: No, I don't want to be your friend.

VERONICA: Why not?

CARSON: I have an idea it's not your strongest suit.

VERONICA: Not just friends, no. *(Pause)* I'll call a taxi then.

CARSON: You have any other ideas?

(A pause as Veronica takes this in.)

VERONICA: How about a foot rub? Let's get these shoes off.

(She undoes CARSON's shoes and takes them off. She rubs her feet. The scene is wordless but slow.)

CARSON: How about a back rub?

(They both take their sweaters off. Carson is quite nervous.)

CARSON: I want you to touch me.

VERONICA: Touch you or fuck you?

CARSON: Fuck me.

(They look at each other and laugh, softly.)

VERONICA: What?

CARSON: You know I half expected the lights to snap out then.

(Blackout)

A Tragedy: San Francisco

ERIN CRESSIDA WILSON

MOLLY and her mother MARIA are in the kitchen. MOLLY is seventeen—half Latina, half Irish-American. MARIA is Latina and about thirty-eight years old. She has AIDS, but is vivacious.

MOLLY is angry. She wears a barber's bib and has black cut wet hair all over her. Her hair is short, like a little boy's. She looks ridiculous. Her mother's husband has just cut and dyed MOLLY's hair black to make her look more Latin. It is MOLLY's parents' idea that this will help her get into college.

A college application sits on the kitchen table. Bill Withers' "Ain't No Sunshine" plays lightly in the next room.

This is a fast and earthy fight between mother and daughter.

MOLLY: He gave me a piece of shit haircut!
MARIA *(Overlapping):* What?!
MOLLY: You heard me.
MARIA: Obviously I heard you.
MOLLY *(Overlapping):* What's that music?
MARIA: What music? Don't say "shit." I don't hear no music.
MOLLY: He's playing seventies music.
MARIA: Don't say that word.
MOLLY: Shit?!
MARIA: Don't say it!
MOLLY: Shit!
MARIA: Ay! Dios mio.
MOLLY *(Overlapping):* Don't talk Mexican.
MARIA: Spanish!

MOLLY *(Overlapping):* Who does that asshole think he is!

MARIA: He's your father for Christ's sakes!

MOLLY: My STEPfather!

MARIA: Your father!

MOLLY: My father had red hair!

MARIA: Watch it!

MOLLY: Not black hair! Why do I have to have black hair, Mom! Why did you dye it black?!

MARIA: That's enough!

MOLLY: He's an asshole!

MARIA: Get out!

MOLLY: Don't!

MARIA: Come here!

MOLLY: Don't talk like that.

MARIA: Come here.

MOLLY: Don't tell me "get out" then "come here."

MARIA: Come here.

MOLLY: Don't tell me that!

MARIA: Stop it. I hear you.

MOLLY *(Overlapping):* Shut up!

MARIA: Shut up!

> *(Pause. MOLLY turns to the college application that sits in front of her.)*

MARIA: Check the box.

MOLLY: Which box?

MARIA: "Other." And use my maiden name.

MOLLY: Where?

MARIA: You got "black," you got "white," and you got "other." And use my maiden name.

MOLLY: Garcia Rivera Valenzuela de la Riva?

MARIA: You'll get into school.

MOLLY: They ask for a picture.

MARIA: You look Mexican enough.

MOLLY: Mom! I used to look so fine before.

MARIA: That's stupid, you know it.

MOLLY: I know it's stupid. But I look like somebody else now. I look like anybody else now. I look like a fucking Cholo Mission Street geek. Who am I? I hate it. Fuck. Mom!

MARIA: It's beautiful hair.

MOLLY: What did you marry a fucking hairdresser for?

MARIA: Here, you keep the hair, you keep the hair, remember the hair.

(MARIA starts picking up the hair and putting it into MOLLY's arms.)

MOLLY: I look like fucking Frida Kahlo.

MARIA: I'll cut my hair like you.

MOLLY: He took my power, he took my edge. He said it would be OK. It's not OK.

MARIA: Give me the scissors.

(MOLLY turns back to the application. MARIA starts to cut a bit of her own hair off herself.)

MOLLY: Mom, what's my hobbies?

MARIA: Say Amnesty International. You're a volunteer for Amnesty International.

MOLLY: What?

MARIA *(Overlapping):* Say it!

MOLLY: No!

MARIA: Write it!

MOLLY: I won't!

MARIA: Now!

(She writes it.)

MOLLY: How about clubs?

MARIA: What?

MOLLY: Sports.

MARIA: Put tennis, too.

MOLLY: Jesus Christ.

MARIA: A Mexican tennis player, you volunteer for Amnesty, you'll get in.

MOLLY: You always said I was Irish.

MARIA: So what, that's what I said.

MOLLY: You named me O'Connor, Dad's name.

MARIA: Your dad's gone.

MOLLY: Then why didn't you give me YOUR last name? Why did you give me HIS name and why did you THEN name me Molly? You gave me an Irish name, Mom. Obviously.

MARIA: I thought it would help you. But now it won't help you.

MOLLY: Why?

MARIA: Molly Garcia Rivera Valenzuela de la Riva, and we're making it legal! Here, take this lock. Keep it. (*MARIA hands MOLLY a lock of her hair.*)

MOLLY: What do you want me to do with it?

MARIA: Put it in a locket, how the fuck do I know. Keep it somewhere special.

MOLLY: OK.

MARIA: That's good. That's good.

MOLLY: But I hate the name Garcia Rivera Valenzuela de la Riva! And besides you've always told me you were from Spain. Your family was from Spain? What did you think that was gonna help?

MARIA: What?

MOLLY: Madrid!

MARIA: Get on with the application!

MOLLY: What? Now you're from Mexico? Or should I just write down Nicaragua, they might like that, or better yet, Sarejevo!

MARIA: Change it! I got the white out!

MOLLY: No!

(*MARIA comes and tears up the application.*)

MOLLY: Mom!

MARIA: Don't go to school then!

MOLLY: You can't lie on these things!

MARIA: It's not a lie, you're a Mexican God damn it. That's no lie and that's gonna get you somewhere. WITH a scholarship!

MOLLY: Why?

MARIA: The cycle's done.

MOLLY: What cycle?

MARIA: You are no longer grateful for the toilet paper and the dollars in your pocket, you're no longer thankful for the smell of American soap and towels and papers inside the books and

the fine print, you already know all this, this is nothing,
you're an American . . . here . . . wait . . . check . . . there . . .
American Indian, write Native American.

(MARIA *hands* MOLLY *another application.*)

MOLLY: What?

MARIA: That's what we are, Native American, before the Spanish
got in our blood, we were Indians, so put down Native
American.

MOLLY: Which one is this?

MARIA: The Stanford one, fuck Berkeley.

A Knife in the Heart

SUSAN YANKOWITZ

MRS. HOLT's only son, Donald, has murdered the Governor of New York. In a state of mingled grief, guilt, and compassion, she goes to see the mother of the victim. MRS. HOLT stands alone in a pool of light. Then she puts on her black hat with the mourning veil pushed back. She walks to a door that now becomes visible. She raises her hand to the ornate knocker, then hesitates. She composes herself and does knock. The door opens. MRS. DIAMOND, leaning on a cane, dressed in the same black dress and hat as MRS. HOLT, stands there. In tense silence, they confront each other.

MRS. DIAMOND: And why are *you* dressed in black, Mrs. Holt?

MRS. HOLT: I too have lost a son, Mrs. Diamond.

MRS. DIAMOND: Will you sit down?

MRS. HOLT: Will you?

MRS. DIAMOND: I'd prefer not.

MRS. HOLT: It's very kind of you to see me.

MRS. DIAMOND: I see you.

MRS. HOLT: You look at me the way I look at myself—when I can bear to look at all.

MRS. DIAMOND: We both have our afflictions.

MRS. HOLT: You make it very difficult, Mrs. Diamond. . . . But I had to come. I want to tell you that I'm sorry—

MRS. DIAMOND: How original of you, Mrs. Holt.

MRS. HOLT: —more than sorry! I'm pained, anguished, heart-sick—poor words, I know, to describe these feelings, but . . . what else do we have?

MRS. DIAMOND: We? Please. Don't include me in your general-izations.

MRS. HOLT: No one knows better than I what you must be suffering.

MRS. DIAMOND: Brava. Now that's off your chest, you must feel better.

MRS. HOLT: No, I don't. I didn't come for that.

MRS. DIAMOND: Quite right. If you want absolution, go to your priest.

MRS. HOLT: I don't have a priest, Mrs. Diamond. All I have is hell. And you're there with me, I know you are. I feel you breathing next to me as we walk under that hail of fire. I think of *my* boy—and I weep for yours. I listen again and again to the sounds of my baby's laughter, that sweet music, and I hear your boy's laughter, too—and it goes on, ringing in my ears, night after night, like a death bell pealing for both of them, for both of us.

MRS. DIAMOND: Spare me your odious comparisons.

MRS. HOLT: I can't. Our sons are linked together, now and forever. Yours is the martyr, mine the traitor. Yours is the hero, mine the scum. You have that, at least.

MRS. DIAMOND: I didn't want the least, Mrs. Holt. My son was the best this country had to offer. The best!

MRS. HOLT: I would trade places with you if I could! How much better to be the mother of the crucified one than to have borne the man who hammered in the nails!

MRS. DIAMOND: Better? Better to have ripped that life out of you with a coat hanger!

MRS. HOLT: No!

MRS. DIAMOND: You dare say 'no'?

MRS. HOLT: I do say it, I do. Look. *(Pulling photographs from her purse)* I insist that you look!

(She forces them in front of MRS. DIAMOND's eyes.)

Here's Donald at six months, with his three new teeth. Here he is at a year, taking his first steps. This is Donald at two. He could recite every nursery rhyme in his book. Don't look away. I want you to see. This is the boy you hate. This is the boy you want to kill. He idolized your son. At every rally,

Donald was there. When the Governor spoke on television, Donald was watching. Some boys have pinups on their walls. My boy had pictures of your Philip.

MRS. DIAMOND: Stop it! Do you hear? Don't tell me any more about your son's perversities!

(She raises her cane and brings it down on the frame of the sofa, just beside MRS. HOLT. A framed photograph of Philip falls to the floor and the glass breaks.)

There! Now you've destroyed something else! First your son—then mine. And now this! How dare you walk into this house with your excuses! How dare you ask that I forgive you! Live with your torment, Mrs. Holt, as I live with mine. Have some dignity, at least. Now go away. Get out. Leave my home.

MRS. HOLT: You think your son's photograph is worth more than mine? Your memories more than mine? Yes, that's how it is with aristocrats! Even your grief is better than ours. Tell me, Mrs. Diamond: do you save your excrement for your archives?

(MRS. DIAMOND slaps her. MRS. HOLT traps the hand against her cheek.)

Feel, Mrs. Diamond, feel. Skin. Real flesh. Wrinkles, like yours. Blood underneath, like yours.

(She forces the hand to her breast.)

Breasts that gave milk to my child.

(She forces the hand to her belly.)

A womb that grew full. A stomach scarred with stretch marks.

(She forces the hand between her legs.)

A vagina, like yours. Remember? This is where his head pushed out!

(She releases MRS. DIAMOND's hand.)

I loved my son. I'll love him forever. That's what fate has forced on me. That's my dignity, Mrs. Diamond.

(MRS. DIAMOND stands frozen. Then she kneels abruptly and begins picking up the shards of broken glass. MRS. HOLT doesn't move. MRS. DIAMOND cries out as her hand is cut on the glass.)

MRS. DIAMOND: Oh!

MRS. HOLT *(Hesitating, then removing her mourning veil):* Give me your hand, Mrs. Diamond.

(Silently, she wraps the black gauze around MRS. DIAMOND's bleeding hand.)

MRS. DIAMOND: Thank you.

(She sits down on the sofa where MRS. HOLT had been. MRS. HOLT kneels and continues picking up the glass. Lights dim.)

Thirteen Rites

WENDY YONDORF

The living room of an apartment in Chicago. CAMILLE, age 13, is Hispanic. A Jewish family adopted her seven years ago and still regards her as a misfit. She is street-smart and tough. LILLITH, age 12, is a straight-A student and knows nothing about the real world. It is the day before LILLITH's Bat Mitzvah. The girls are cousins, though not by blood. They have only met each other once, five years earlier.

LILLITH: Hi. *(Pause)* Do you have a rubber band?

CAMILLE: No.

LILLITH: I lost my covered rubber band I got in Israel and—

CAMILLE: Yeah, so?

LILLITH: Where do you live?

CAMILLE: Seattle.

LILLITH: I was there once. It's a lot smaller than Chicago. And we went from there to Canada and Japan.

CAMILLE: So?

LILLITH: Me and my friends—I mean, my friends and I—we like to meet and swap stuff. Like I gave Rebecca some of my hair and she gave me a handkerchief of her father's.

CAMILLE: Huh.

LILLITH: It's a white one and it's got "Sears" printed on it.

(CAMILLE pulls out some chewing gum and slowly unwraps a piece for herself.)

Can I have a piece?

CAMILLE: I guess so. Here. *(Hands LILLITH a piece.)* I still have one more. Aren't your parents like my Grandma Louise's age?

LILLITH: Yeah. They got married late.

CAMILLE: How come?

LILLITH: I don't know. I have to work on my presentation for tomorrow.

CAMILLE: How long are you gonna stay here?

LILLITH: We met once before.

CAMILLE: I doubt it.

LILLITH: Your dad and mom and my mom and my dad and you and I went to the Carlsbad Caverns in Texas.

CAMILLE: Oh yeah! There was bat crap all over the place.

LILLITH: And you touched it. The crap.

CAMILLE: I remember that, I don't remember you though.

LILLITH: So, do you really have something in your arm to control sex?

CAMILLE: That's not what it does!

LILLITH: I knew that. *(Pause)* How big is it, I mean, does it hurt when they insert it?

CAMILLE: It's called Norplant, you idiot, and, no, it doesn't hurt.

LILLITH: I knew that . . . Why do you have to . . . ? *(Pause)* Are you going to have a confirmation?

CAMILLE: No way! . . . What's that?

LILLITH: Well, because I'm Jewish, I'm having a Bat Mitzvah and tomorrow I get to say the Haftarah and I also get to do a Devortorah, but in most Christian churches, I think the girls have confirmations and they give their souls to Jesus or something.

CAMILLE: Yeah, I might.

LILLITH: Eww! I don't like long hair on boys. There's this boy in my Hebrew class, Saul Silverstein, who is mega cute. He's my same height and I do his math homework for him. He's in a lower math class than me. His class is still doing like multiplication and we're doing percentages and set theory. But he plays the flute really well.

CAMILLE: I play the piano.

LILLITH: Me too. I'm working on this Chopin piece, it's really hard.

CAMILLE: Huh. Can you play "Chopsticks"?

LILLITH *(Blurts out):* Did you go all the way?!

CAMILLE: Yeah.

LILLITH: OH MY GOD!

CAMILLE: Shut up dummy!

LILLITH: Oh wow, oh wow, oh wow!

CAMILLE: All right! You can ask me two questions. And that's it.

LILLITH: OK. Wait. I don't know what to ask first! Wait. Um. Oh! Well, OK. How long, I mean, how long, after it goes in—right?—how long does it stay in?

CAMILLE: About . . . three, maybe four seconds.

LILLITH: Gross!

CAMILLE: It is sorta gross.

LILLITH: There's this girl in my school, Elise Cocke, and she's into lay-making.

CAMILLE: Huh. What's that?

LILLITH: Well, I think, you're lying down, like on a couch, while you're making out. *(Pause)* Was it really gross?

CAMILLE: Not really. It feels like . . .

LILLITH: What?

CAMILLE: Like . . .

LILLITH: What?!

CAMILLE: Like nothing.

LILLITH: Wow. Can I feel that patch?

CAMILLE: Sure.

> *(LILLITH touches CAMILLE's arm.)*

LILLITH: That is so weird! Does your boyfriend have to wear one too?

> *(CAMILLE looks distant, removed. LILLITH notices.)*

You don't have to talk about it.

CAMILLE: It's no big deal! I just wish I could talk to my mama.

LILLITH: You talk to your mom about that stuff?!

CAMILLE: I don't mean my mom, she just adopted me. I mean my real whole mom.

LILLITH: Oh.

CAMILLE: Booboo and Edgar never have sex. That's why they

adopted me. My real mama is really beautiful and rich and she lives in Mexico–I mean Hawaii. She has a horse farm with about a hundred dogs.

LILLITH: Have you been to Israel?

CAMILLE: Nuh-uh. Mama's name is Esmeralda. You wanna try and channel her?

LILLITH: What's that?

CAMILLE: If you lie down, I'll see if I can like get her to speak through you.

LILLITH: Oh, come on. How?

CAMILLE: Here, light that candle. Wait, I got a light.

LILLITH: Why don't we just call her in Hawaii?

CAMILLE: No! This is better.

(CAMILLE grabs a candle from the room, pulls some matches out of her pocket and hands them to LILLITH who lights the candle.)

Now lie down.

LILLITH: I'm NOT lying on the floor. I'll get germs and pneumonia.

CAMILLE: On the couch. Lie on the couch. Just lie down! *(LILLITH does.)* OK, relax. Wait, I'm gonna turn off the lights.

(CAMILLE flips off the overhead light and kneels at one end of the couch by LILLITH's head.)

LILLITH: I thought you only channel dead people.

CAMILLE: No, it's for long distance, too. OK. Relax. Close your eyes. Keep 'em closed! OK. You're walking down the beach—

LILLITH: I'm allergic to sand.

CAMILLE: Shhh! You can't talk. OK. You're walking down the beach and the sand is like warm baby powder. And you're wearing a green silk dress and everybody—

LILLITH: Why am I wearing a green silk dress?

CAMILLE: Cuz you are! And everybody is staring at you. And you stop by a palm tree and—

LILLITH: —to get some coconut milk!

(LILLITH and CAMILLE dissolve in laughter.)

CAMILLE: OK, OK, OK! Shhh. The milk is really cold and your feet are hot hot hot—

LILLITH: So I pour the milk on my feet. *(More laughter)*

CAMILLE: OK. Shut up! Now. Close your eyes! OK, you're walking down the beach and the sand is like warm baby powder. And you're wearing a green silk dress. And you see your daughter walking toward you. Slowly. And she's got on a black silk dress and she gets closer and closer and you raise up your arm . . . you raise up your arm . . .

> *(CAMILLE punches LILLITH when she doesn't pick up her cue. LILLITH raises her arm, stretches it out, and slowly waves her hand, "hello." CAMILLE giggles at this.)*

. . . and you wave, "hello." And she doesn't see you in the hot hot sun with your hot hot feet. And you call to her—

> *(LILLITH suddenly sounds and acts like a fantasy mother. Her interpretation is romantic, eerie.)*

LILLITH: Who's there?

CAMILLE: No! *I* say that. You say, I mean, you call to me—

LILLITH: Camille! Camiiiiillle! I've been looking and searching for you.

CAMILLE: Are you the voice of Esmeralda La Plata Gonzalez?

LILLITH: I am, I am!

CAMILLE: Well, say something!

LILLITH: Hi. Hi.

CAMILLE: Why did you leave me?

LILLITH: You were just a baby, and, and I went to buy some coconut milk and this man took you away!

CAMILLE: Why didn't you run after him?

LILLITH: I did. I did. Only you, only you.

CAMILLE: Lillith! Stop saying everything twice.

LILLITH: I brought you a horse. *(She neighs and whinnies.)*

CAMILLE *(Disgusted):* You're not doing it right. This is stupid.

> *(CAMILLE starts to rise; lightning and booming thunder. CAMILLE starts and LILLITH, inhabited by another spirit, speaks in perfect Spanish.)*

LILLITH: Estoy en la voz de Esmeralda La Plata! Forgive me, forgive meeeeee!

(LILLITH's body levitates slowly, up and off the couch about two feet. CAMILLE screams, makes the sign of the cross with both hands.)

CAMILLE: Mama!

Appendix

*Additional Scenes for Women, by Women
Readily Available in the United States
and Britain*

Comic Scenes for Two Women

Abingdon Square by Maria Irene Fornes, Act 1, scene 5. Two young girls talk about sex.

Alice in Bed by Susan Sontag, scene 2. A nurse talks to her patient.

And the Soul Shall Dance by Wakako Yamauchi, Act 2, scene 3. Two Japanese girls—one born in America and one newly immigrated—practice English.

The Conduct of Life by Maria Irene Fornes, scene 4. A power struggle between a maid and her employer.

Crimes of the Heart by Beth Henley, Act 2, after Babe exits. Two sisters talk about childhood injustices and revenge.

Fefu and Her Friends by Maria Irene Fornes, Part II "In the Lawn." Two women talk and play croquet.

Getting Out by Marsha Norman, Act 1, the scene between Arlene and her mother. A mother visits her ex-con daughter.

Getting Out by Marsha Norman, Act 2, the scene between Ruby and Arlene. A recently released convict and her ex-con neighbor talk about reentering the real world.

The Grace of Mary Traverse by Timberlake Wertenbaker, Act 1, scene 2. A woman and her maid struggle for power.

I Love You, I Love You Not by Wendy Kesselman, scene 2. A girl and her grandmother discuss young love.

Isn't It Romantic? by Wendy Wasserstein, Act 2, scene 3. Mother and daughter discuss marriage and children.

The Kathy and Mo Show: Parallel Lives by Mo Gaffney and Kathy Najimy, "Annette and Ginger." Two girls discuss men and dating.

The Kathy and Mo Show: Parallel Lives by Mo Gaffney and Kathy Najimy, "Las Hermanas." Two middle-aged Jewish women in a continuing education class on feminism visit a Hispanic feminist restaurant.

Love of the Nightingale by Timberlake Wertenbaker, scene 2. Sisters talk about men and the mechanics of sexual intercourse.

Machinal by Sophie Treadwell, Episode 2. A mother urges her daughter to get married.

A Member of the Wedding by Carson McCullers, Act 1, the scene between Berenice and Frankie (from "I've got a splinter" to "I wish I had some good cold peach ice cream."). Young girl brags and makes plans for the future with her nurse.

The Miss Firecracker Contest by Beth Henley, scene 1 until the entrance of Elain. Young girl and her seamstress talk about beauty contests and comic family tragedies.

My Mother Said I Never Should by Charlotte Keatley, Act 1, scene 3. Two young girls try to understand birth.

The Oldest Profession by Paula Vogel, scene after the third blackout. Two elderly whores discuss how the death of a third affects their business.

Playhouse Creatures by April DeAngelis, Act 1, scene 1. Nell Gwynn inadvertently tells Elizabeth Farley about an available role at the theatre.

Third and Oak by Marsha Norman, Act 1 opening. Deedee and Alberta meet in a laundromat.

Top Girls by Caryl Churchill, Act 2, scene 3, "Interview." A woman interviews for a job.

When I Was Girl I Used to Scream and Shout by Sharman Macdonald, "1960 Bedroom." Mother and daughter discuss masturbation.

When I Was Girl I Used to Scream and Shout by Sharman Macdonald, "1961 Bedroom." Two girls discuss sex and divorce.

Why We Have A Body by Claire Chafee, Act 1, scene 11. Two women in a plane discuss sexuality.

The Women by Clare Booth, scene 6. The cook and the maid discuss the marriage and divorce of their employer.

Comic Scenes for Three Women

The Grace of Mary Traverse by Timberlake Wertenbaker, Act 3, scene 4. A rich city girl, a country girl, and a maid try to understand each other as they dream of a new world.

Heidi Chronicles by Wendy Wasserstein, Act 2, scene 3. Three women have lunch and learn how they've grown apart.

Once a Catholic by Mary O'Malley, Act 1, scene 8. Catholic school girls discuss the facts of life.

Queen Christina by Pam Gems, Act 2, scene 1. Queen Christina of Sweden shocks two French ladies at tea.

Sisters by Patricia Montley, Act 2, scene 2. A woman considers having sex.

Dramatic Scenes for Two Women

The Children's Hour by Lillian Hellman, Act 2, scene 1. A young girl tells her grandmother a lie.

Desdemona by Paul Vogel, scenes 26, 27, and 28. A queen and her maid discuss marriage.

Fen by Caryl Churchill, scene 19. A mother tortures her daughter, who still loves her.

Gut Girls by Sarah Daniels, Act 1, scene 7. Mother and daughter discuss motherhood.

Isn't It Romantic? by Wendy Wasserstein, Act 2, scene 5. Two old friends discuss marriage and loneliness.

Jar the Floor by Cheryl West, Act 2, scene 3. A young woman and her friend's great-grandmother discuss marriage and pain.

The Little Foxes by Lillian Hellman, Act 3, the scene between Alexandra and Birdie. An older woman passes on wisdom about survival techniques to her niece.

Ma Rose by Cassandra Medley, Act 2, scene 1. A mother and daughter discuss an aging grandmother.

Masterpieces by Sarah Daniels, scene 4. A social worker tries to help a prostitute.

Miriam's Flowers by Migdalia Cruz, scene 2. A daughter tries to convince her mother that her son is dead.

My Mother Said I Never Should by Charlotte Keatley, Act 1, scene 2. A mother puts her child to bed on Christmas during World War II.

My Mother Said I Never Should by Charlotte Keatley, Act 2, scene 1. A mother and her middle-aged daughter discuss marriage.

My Sister in This House by Wendy Kesselman, Act 1, scene 2. Two sisters are reunited.

Our Country's Good by Timberlake Wertenbaker, Act 1, scene 8, until Liz's entrance. Two women discuss the nature of virginity and the need to survive.

Pax by Deborah Levy, Act 1, scene 1. The keeper of a large house welcomes a strange guest.

Plumes by Georgia Douglas Johnson, complete. A woman tries to decide whether to use her limited money for surgery or a funeral for her daughter.

A Raisin in the Sun by Lorraine Hansberry, Act 1, scene 1. A woman tries to convince her mother-in-law to give her son some money.

Sally's Shorts by Sally Nemeth, "The Cat Act." A nurse does physical therapy with a stroke patient.

Sarita by Maria Irene Fornes, Act 1, scene 2. A daughter tells her mother that she's pregnant.

Signs of Life by Joan Schenkar, "Alice's Room." Alice James and her companion discuss love and writing.

Taste of Honey by Shelagh Delaney, Act 1, scene 1, until Peter's entrance. Mother and daughter argue in a new apartment.

Taste of Honey by Shelagh Delaney, Act 1, scene 2, after Boy's exit. Mother and daughter go their separate ways.

Trifles by Sarah Glaspell, throughout. Two women discuss a murder investigation.

Dramatic Scenes for Three Women

And the Soul Shall Dance by Wakako Yamauchi, Act 2, scene 5. A mother and daughter admire kimonos but cannot afford to buy them.

Beside Herself by Sarah Daniels, scene 8. Two women discuss sexual abuse.

Etta Jenks by Marlane Meyer, scene 7. Three strippers discuss dematerializing.

The Stick Wife by Darrah Cloud, Act 1, scene 2. Three women exchange news of a racist bombing.

Top Girls by Caryl Churchill, Act 3, scene 4. Two sisters discuss motherhood and careers.

Biographies

DALE ELIZABETH ATTIAS is an award-winning poet and playwright. She began in theatre first as an actress, then as a costume designer. Ms. Attias developed many of her plays, including *Perfect Light,* in conjunction with the Santa Cruz Actors' Theatre.

JILL IRIS BACHARACH received an M.A. in writing from the University of San Francisco and an M.S.W. from Yeshiva University. After participating in the Padua Hills Playwrights Festival in Los Angeles, she trained in acting. *Boulder Rock* was inspired by Paul Gauguin's painting entitled *Nevermore.* She is currently working on a collection of poems.

SALLIE BINGHAM moved to the Southwest in 1991, and since then has published three novels with Zoland Books: *Small Victories, Matron of Honor,* and *Straight Man.* These novels are her farewell to the South, which she also portrayed in her first novel, *After Such Knowledge,* two collections of short stories, and a memoir. Her plays have been produced by The Women's Project and Productions in New York City as well as by regional theatres.

ROSE CARUSO received the 1995 Jane Chambers Playwriting Award and the 1996 Source Theatre's Literary Prize for *Shamanism in New Jersey.* Some of her other plays are *Love and Roadkill,* presented at the Source Theatre; *One with God, Two with a Guest,* presented at the New Jersey Theatre Festival; *Chemo Buddies,* commissioned by Smallbeer Theatre Company in Washington, DC, and produced by 12 Miles West in Montclair, NJ; *Tuning In,* a musical commissioned by George Street Playhouse; *The First Light Home,* developed at the Midwest Playlabs Conference, presented at Ensemble Studio Theatre's Octoberfest, and produced at Virginia Tech; and *Suffering Heart Salon,* which received the Writer's Digest First Place Award, an artist's fellowship from the New York Foundations of the Arts, and the Beverly Hills Theatre Guild Playwright's Award.

NANCY S. CHU is a director, writer, and performer in New York, producing numerous works in her career. Having graduated with honors from Trinity College in Hartford, CT, she studied theatre in Moscow and Bulgaria, then worked with companies in the United States, such as Company One (Hartford) and Mabou Mines (New York). She is also a member of the Lincoln Center Theater Directors Lab (New York). Many of the works she has directed are new plays, written by herself and other emerging playwrights; movement-oriented performance pieces created by an ensemble cast; or adaptations of children's folktales.

LAURA EDMONDSON is a Ph.D. candidate in theatre history and criticism at the University of Texas at Austin. *Composing Tchaikovsky*, which received its first production in October 1997 at Tulane University, has also been entered into the American College Theatre Festival.

LINDA EISENSTEIN's plays include *Three the Hard Way* (winner, Gilmore Creek Playwriting Competition), *Marla's Devotion* (Festival Prize, All England Theatre Festival), and *The Names of the Beast* (winner, Sappho's Symposium Competition, Jane Chambers Award honors). She has received two Ohio Arts Council fellowships, and an OAC new works commission for her opera *Street Sense* with Migdalia Cruz. She is a member of the Cleveland Play House Playwrights Unit. Her work has been performed on three continents.

ANNIE EVANS' plays have been produced at such theatres as the New York Stage and Film Company, Manhattan Class Company, Actors Theatre of Louisville, Circle Repertory Company Lab, Ensemble Studio Theatre, and the Eugene O'Neill National Playwrights Conference, among others. Ms. Evans is a writer on the acclaimed children's show *Sesame Street* (Emmy nomination) as well as several other children's shows on PBS, Nickelodeon, and the Discovery Channel. She is a 1984 graduate of Brown University.

MICHELLE A. GABOW is a playwright and educator in the Boston area. Five of her full-length plays (*Prozac's Sister, Who Killed Martha Mitchell, Knock Knock, The Lunch*, and *Parima*) and a video drama (*Queen of Swords*) have been produced in Boston. Presently, she is the co-artistic director of The Women's Theatre Project, a troupe dedicated to cross-cultural, experimental, feminist, and affordable theatre.

MARY FENGAR GAIL's plays include *Planet of the Mutagens, Carnivals of Desire, Lord Velvet,* and *Jambulu.* Her work has been developed at the Sundance Institute Playwrights Lab, the New York Stage and Film Company, and the Eugene O'Neill National Playwrights Conference. She is a recipient of the Arnold Weissberger Award, the Stanley Drama Award, and the National Children's Theatre Festival Award. *Fuchsia* was a winner of the Center Theatre Ensemble's International Playwriting Competition.

LAURA HARRINGTON's plays and musicals have been produced regionally, off Broadway, and in Canada. Some recent credits include: *The Perfect 36,* Tennessee Repertory Theatre; *Joan of Arc,* Boston Music Theatre Project; *Marathon Dancing,* En Garde Arts (New York) and in Munich, Germany; *Martin Guerre,* Hartford Stage Company; *Lucy's Lapses,* Portland Opera Company, and Playwrights' Horizons; *Hearts on Fire,* New Music Theatre Ensemble, Minneapolis; *Babes in Toyland,* Houston Grand Opera; and a feminist adaptation of *Sleeping Beauty,* North Shore Music Theatre in Massachusetts. Ms. Harrington is on the faculty at M.I.T. Awards include a Bunting Institute Fellowship, a Whiting Foundation Grant, a Massachusetts Cultural Council Award for Playwriting, the Joseph Kesselring Award for Drama, Opera America development and commissioning grants, a New England Emmy, and a Quebec Cinematique Award.

NAOMI IIZUKA's most recent play, *Polaroid Stories,* was commissioned by En Garde Arts and produced in the 1997 Humana Festival at the Actors Theatre of Louisville. Other plays include *Scheherazade, Skin,* and *Tattoo Girl.* Ms. Iizuka is the recipient of a McKnight Advancement Grant and a Jerome Playwriting Fellowship. She received her B.A. from Yale University and her M.F.A. from the University of California–San Diego.

CORINNE JACKER's plays include *The Island* and *In the Dark,* Georgia Repertory; an American version of Chekhov's *Three Sisters* and an adaptation of *Hedda Gabler,* Pittsburgh Public Theatre; *Songs from Distant Lands,* Yale Rep; *Breakfast, Lunch, and Dinner* and *Bits and Pieces* (Obie winner), Primary Stages; and *My Life, Harry Outside* (Obie), *After the Season, Domestic Issues, In Place* (*Best Short Plays of 1984*), *Night Thoughts, Chinese Restaurant Syndrome* (*Best Short Plays of 1977*), and *Terminal,* all first produced at Circle Rep. She has taught playwriting at NYU, Yale, and Princeton, and now teaches film writing at Columbia. Along with her Obies, she has won two Emmy Citations, a Peabody Award, and a Cine Golden Eagle.

SHERRY KRAMER's plays include *The Ruling Passion, Things That Break, The Law Makes Evening Fall, Napoleon's China, The Wall of Water, What A Man Weighs, David's Redhaired Death, The World at Absolute Zero,* and *Partial Objects.* Her works have been produced at Yale Rep, Soho Rep, The Second Stage, Ensemble Studio Theatre, Woolly Mammoth, Signature Theatre, Annex Theatre in Seattle, and other theatres here and abroad. Her awards include those from the NEA, the New York Foundation for the Arts, the McKnight Foundation, and the Pew Charitable Trust. Her plays have won the Weissberger, the Jane Chambers, and the Marvin Taylor Playwriting Awards. She is an alumna of New Dramatists.

ARDEN TERESA LEWIS is a playwright and an actress who has seen her plays *Tabloids, Rex,* and *Little Rhonda* produced on Theatre Row and at the Ohio Theatre in New York. The two-act version of *Little Rhonda* also had a successful run at Theatre Geo in Los Angeles. Her play *Baby Dreams* was included in Theatre West's West Works Festival in Los Angeles and was a finalist for the 1995 Jane Chambers Playwriting Award. Ms. Lewis is co-moderator of Theatre West's Writers Workshop, a graduate of UCLA, and a member of Theatre Geo and the Dramatists Guild.

JESSICA LITWAK's *A Pirate's Lullaby* was produced by The Goodman Theatre and Artists Repertory Theatre in Portland, where it won the Portland Drama Critics Circle's Drammy Award and the Oregon Book Award. Other plays include *Between Wind, Secret Agents, 22 Filmore, The Promised Land,* and *Reincarnation.* Ms. Litwak has performed her one-woman plays *Fire Dreams, Holiday: A Year in the Life,* and *Emma Goldman: Love, Anarchy and Other Affairs* throughout New York and in San Francisco and Portland, Oregon. Ms. Litwak has written for radio and television, and is currently working on her second feature-length screenplay. She has a B.F.A. from N.Y.U. and an M.F.A. from Columbia University.

LISA LOOMER's plays, including *The Waiting Room, Birds, ¡Bocón!, Looking for Angels, Cuts, Maria! Maria, Maria, Maria,* and *Accelerando* have been produced at Mark Taper Forum, Arena Stage, South Coast Repertory, the Kennedy Center, The Public Theater, La Jolla Playhouse, Trinity Repertory, Williamstown Theater Festival, LATC, Vineyard Theater, and The Odyssey. Ms. Loomer has received grants from the NEA and NYPA, is a winner of the American Theater Critics Award and the Jane Chambers Award, and is a runner-up for the Susan Smith Blackburn Prize. She is an alumna of New Dramatists.

HEATHER MCDONALD's *Dream of a Common Language* premiered at Berkeley Repertory Theatre and has had several other productions including one directed by the author at Theatre of the First Amendment. That production was nominated for eight Helen Hayes Awards and won four, including Outstanding Production. Her other plays *An Almost Holy Picture, The Rivers and Ravines, Available Light,* and *Faulkner's Bicycle* have been produced at La Jolla Playhouse, McCarter Theatre, Arena Stage, Yale Repertory Theatre, Actors Theatre of Louisville, and off broadway. She has twice been awarded NEA Playwriting Fellowships.

KATHLEEN MCGHEE-ANDERSON, a graduate of Spelman College and Columbia University, works in television, film, and theatre. Her plays *Oak and Ivy* and *Jump at the Sun!* (New Professional Theatre Award) were developed at the Eugene O'Neill Theater Conference. *Oak and Ivy* premiered at the Crossroads Theater (New Brunswick, NJ), and has been produced by Karamu Theater (Cleveland), Arena Theater (Baltimore), Bushfire Theater (Philadelphia), and Howard University Theater. *Mothers,* commissioned by Bill Cosby and developed in Mark Taper Forum's New Work Festival, premiered at The Crossroads Theater. *Jump at the Sun!* and *Mothers* appeared at L.A. Theater Works and on National Public Radio. Other plays include *Five Mojo Secrets* and *Venice,* both developed through the Mark Taper's Blacksmyths.

REGINA PORTER is an honors graduate of the Dramatic Writing Program at New York University's Tisch School of the Arts. Her play *Mourn in Red* received a grant from the Drama League of New York and won the 1990 John Gassner Award for Outstanding One-Act Play. Her play *Man, Woman, Dinosaur* was commissioned by American Playhouse, workshopped at Playwrights Horizons, and produced at Woolly Mammoth Theatre. She recently completed *A Classic*

Misunderstanding on commission for Actors Theatre of Louisville's Humana Festival. Her play *Tripping Through the Car House* was produced by Woolly Mammoth Theatre Company. She has received a Van Lier Grant from The Women's Project and an Edward Albee Fellowship.

PATRICIA S. SMITH's work has been seen at Woolly Mammoth Theatre, The National Museum of Women in the Arts, the Corcoran Museum, and the Source Theatre where she won Most Outstanding Production in the 1996 New Plays Festival. She has also had productions at Cleveland Public Theatre and Love Creek Productions in New York City and has been a finalist in several national contests, including 1996 honorable mention in the Jane Chambers Playwriting Award for *Designed for Sacrifice*, her first full-length play. Her latest full-length play, *The Butterfly Effect*, applies chaos theory to the DC inner-city.

ARLENE STERNE, actor/playwright, has toured the United States, Canada, England, and Scotland with her prize-winning solo play *Final Curtain* (Torch of Hope Award, New York, 1995; Director's Award, Los Angeles, 1993) and starred in the TV adaptation *Actress Works* for PBS. Her career has taken her to four continents as actor, writer, broadcast journalist, talk show host, and guest artist. She resides in New York and commutes to Los Angeles to work in prime-time television.

JEAN STERRETT was born in Australia. Marriage to a Georgian brought her to Atlanta, where she has combined a career performing and teaching music with forays into the theatre world as an actress, sound designer, director, and playwright. Her body of work, for which she received Atlanta's First Mayor's Fellowship in the Arts Drama Award, includes two musicals and nine plays, two of which, *Afternoons at Waratah* and *The Moebius Band*, have won national awards. Ms. Sterrett is a member of The Dramatists Guild.

CARIDAD SVICH, a playwright and translator of Cuban, Croatian, Argentine, and Spanish descent, is currently a resident playwright at Mark Taper Forum Theatre in Los Angeles. Her play *Alchemy of Desire/Dead-Man's Blues* received its premiere at Cincinnati Playhouse in the Park, as winner of the Rosenthal New Play Prize. It has subsequently been staged in London, Miami, and Edmonton, Alberta. She is now a visiting lecturer at Yale School of Drama. Her essays on theatre have been seen in *American Theatre* and *Contemporary Theatre Review/UK.*

ANASTASIA TRAINA's plays include *Memories are for Coffee, From Riverdale to Riverhead, Natural History,* and *Winnie and G,* all of which were produced by E.S.T. at their October Fest. *Winnie and G,* a finalist in the Samuel French Contest '95, has also been produced by Love Creek on Theatre Row and The Common Basis Theatre. Other theatres that have produced Ms. Traina's plays include the Director's Company, Westbeth, the Hudson Theatre Guild, and Expanded Arts. Ms. Traina is currently working on a new play, *The Broken Branch,* and adapting her play *From Riverdale to Riverhead* into a screenplay.

ALICE TUAN's work, including *Last of the Suns* and *Ikebana,* has been seen at Berkeley Repertory Theater, East West Players, Mark Taper Forum, The Public Theater, and Trinity Repertory Theater. Her play *Some Asians* was one of three winners in the Woman's Playwriting Competition at Perishable Theater. She is a graduate of Brown University's M.F.A. playwriting program where she invented Virtual Hypertext Theater, which simulates computer dynamics in a physical stage space to juxtapose artifice with humanness. For two years, Ms. Tuan developed plays with teenage wards at the California Youth Authority. She has also taught English at the South China Normal University in Guangzhou, China, and in Los Angeles.

ALANA VALENTINE's first play, *Multiple Choice,* was produced by the Australian Theatre for Young People. *Southern Belle* was given a public reading in New York with Martha Plimpton and Frances McDormand in principal roles. In 1996, *Swimming the Globe* was produced in Newcastle, with plans for a tour to Malaysia in 1998. Ms. Valentine's most recent play, *The Conjurers,* premiered at the Playbox Theatre in April 1997. Ms. Valentine is the recipient of a New South Wales State Literary Award, a Churchill Fellowship, and the 1995 ANPC/New Dramatists Award. She lives in Sydney, Australia.

ERIN CRESSIDA WILSON is an internationally produced and award-winning playwright and professor at Duke University. She is the recipient of fellowships from the NEA, the Rockefeller Foundation, and most recently from the North Carolina Arts Council. Her latest play, *Hurricane,* opened this season in Chicago, San Francisco, and Seattle and is published in *The American Poetry Review* and *Theatre Forum Magazine*. She is currently under commission to write two original full-length plays for New York's Playwright's Horizons and Chicago's Steppenwolf Theatre. She is a member of New Dramatists.

SUSAN YANKOWITZ's *Phaedra in Delirium* premiered as a coproduction of The Women's Project and Classic Stage Company. She is the librettist and lyricist of *Slain in the Spirit: The Promise of Jim Jones,* a gospel-and-blues opera with music by Taj Mahal. *1969 Terminal 1996,* her collaboration with Joseph Chaikin and an ensemble of actors, traveled in the U. S. and abroad from 1996 through 1998. Her drama *Night Sky,* first produced by The Women's Project, has been seen throughout the U. S., Europe, and South Africa. Ms. Yankowitz received a Berrilla Kerr Award and has been honored by the NEA, TCG, the Rockefeller Foundation, Guggenheim Foundation, Opera America, the McKnight Foundation, and New York Foundation for the Arts.

WENDY YONDORF is a recipient of a Berilla Kerr Foundation Award for her playwriting, and *The Space Between the Trees,* produced by Niagara University, was nominated by the Kennedy Center American College Theatre Festival as a regional finalist. Her one-acts, *The Last Twin* and *8 Across,* were produced by Circle Lab and Westside Arts Theatres in New York City. She comes to playwriting after fifteen years of acting on stage, in film, television, stand-up comedy, and voice-overs. She is presently working on a farce, *Murder in the Book Club.*

Performance Rights

Every effort has been made to contact copyright holders for permission to reprint borrowed material where necessary, but if any oversights have occurred, we would be happy to rectify them in future printings of this work.

c/o Heinemann, 361 Hanover Street, Portsmouth, NH 03801–3912:
Dale Elizabeth Attias
Jill Iris Bacharach
Sallie Bingham
Nancy S. Chu
Laura Edmondson
Michelle A. Gabow
Naomi Iizuka
Arden Teresa Lewis
Patricia S. Smith
Jean Sterrett

Rose Caruso
c/o Bruce Ostler
Bret Adams Agency
448 West 44th Street
New York, NY 10036

Linda Eisenstein
c/o Herone Press
P.O. Box 749
Cleveland, OH 44107–0749

Annie Evans
c/o Betsy Heel
William Morris Agency
1325 Avenue of the Americas
New York, NY 10019

Mary Fengar Gail
c/o Jason Fogelson
William Morris Agency
1325 Avenue of the Americas
New York, NY 10019

Laura Harrington
c/o Mary Harden
Harden/Curtis Associates
850 7th Avenue #405
New York, NY 10019

Corinne Jacker
c/o Judy Boals
Berman, Boals & Flynn
225 Lafayette Suite 1207
New York, NY 10012

Sherry Kramer
c/o Bruce Ostler
Bret Adams Agency
448 West 44th Street
New York, NY 10036

Jessica Litwak
c/o Bruce Ostler
Bret Adams Agency
448 West 44th Street
New York, NY 10036

Lisa Loomer
c/o Peter Hagan
The Gersh Agency
130 West 42nd Street
New York, NY 10036

Heather McDonald
c/o Peregrine Whittlsey
345 East 80th Street #31F
New York, NY 10021

Kathleen McGhee-Anderson
c/o John P. Schmitt
1133 Avenue of the Americas
New York, NY 10036–6710

Regina Porter
c/o Jason Fogelson
William Morris Agency
1325 Avenue of the Americas
New York, NY 10019

Arlene Sterne
c/o Bertha Klausner
International Ltd.
71 Park Avenue
New York, NY 10016

Caridad Svich
c/o Mark Taper Forum
LTI Office
Los Angeles, CA 90012

Anastasia Traina
c/o Frist Artists
ATTN: Richard Picerni
130 West 57th Street
New York, NY 10019

Alice Tuan
c/o Joyce Ketay
1501 Broadway #1908
New York, NY 10036

Alana Valentine
c/o Peregrine Whittlsey
345 East 80th Street #31F
New York, NY 10021

Eric Cressida Wilson
c/o George Lane
William Morris Agency
1325 Avenue of the Americas
New York, NY 10019

Susan Yankowitz
c/o Mary Harden
Harden/Curtis Associates
850 7th Avenue #405
New York, NY 10019

Wendy Yondorf
c/o Ronald Gwiazda
Rosenstone/Wender
3 East 48th Street
New York, NY 10017